EMBRACEABLE ME

Life's Transformation
through a Journey Inward

Inge Maskun

Inge Maskun

ISBN-13: 978-0692419946 (Custom)
ISBN-10: 0692419942

Library of Congress Control Number: 2015905617
Owning My Future, LLC. Duluth, Minnesota.

Printed in the United States of America

ଽୠ୰

To

My Dad and Brother
who raised me with wisdom

S.P.
who continuously
helps me spread my wings

ଽୠ୰

CONTENTS

Inge Maskun

Inge Maskun

৪০০৪

"And you?
When will you begin
that long journey
into yourself?"

Rumi

৪০ ০৪

AS WE BEGIN

Life *is* a journey.

For most of us, our journey started as part of other people's; our parents', our family's. Imagine we're on a train to somewhere, a destination we're not sure about; but our parents most probably are. I was one of those children. I was just happy to be traveling with my parents and brothers, not to be left behind. They promised me this would be a journey we were taking together, a wonderful one we would never forget, "You can achieve anything you want. Explore, and learn well." My mind started dancing cheerfully; expectations traveled faster, creating every dream imaginable.

Then we reached our first stop; we got off and explored. My parents were right, it was an exciting world I encountered at this stop. I learned the first lesson in the school of life; meeting new people other than those I knew well, my family. I started adding color to my life. But something suddenly got in the way, our journey together was disrupted. I was rushed to get back on the train while some family members had to stay behind. I got

5

on the train with the rest. The train was on its way to the next stop, I was dragged along. I passed stop after stop along the way; and somehow my journey didn't seem to be as exciting as I thought it would be, but I went along anyway. Life continued. I adjusted. I drifted through life while the bag I carried was becoming heavier after every stop.

Then one day, I heard a gentle call whisper in my ear, reminding me of the journey that was once introduced to me; the one that was wrapped with a promise it would be unforgettable. I have been on this life train for a while now. Am I going to let myself be dragged along to its final destination and accept this journey as it is? Or, am I going to be a part of it? I can create my own journey now, if I want to. And I can *make from* it; I just have to get on with it, be a part of it. It's most probably going to be a long and winding journey, but it'll be worth it.

The calling is getting louder ..."so, when?" it asks me.

The start of our road trip ...

Inge Maskun

ഇൗൽ

*"It was
the most amazing feeling
in the world
to know that something right
happened, and to know
that it had happened
not through luck or command
but simply because
it was right."*

David Levithan
Wide Awake

ഇൽ

1

SURPRISES 700 MILES AWAY FROM HOME

The car glided slowly through a dark brick street and finally stopped at the beginning of the roundabout. We finally found the Bed & Breakfast we were staying in for the next four nights after circling the area for fifteen minutes. The streets were poorly marked and we kept missing the street we were supposed to turn into. It was almost eight o'clock, the neighborhood was dark and drizzly wet. We got out of the car, stretched our legs and moved around the car slowly before we approached the front porch. We had been on the road close to twelve hours, the trip was considerably smooth. Physically, I felt well and I was pleasantly surprised I felt as well emotionally.

My husband and I took turns driving, when we left our home at the western tip of Lake Superior, the weather was hazy and gloomy. It was typical November weather. He drove through Minnesota. I took over the wheel and drove through Iowa and the northern tip of Kansas. I was hoping for warmer weather in Pittsburg but it didn't look like it would be, it was as subdued and gloomy as it was at home. I can't complain. I'd been blessed with great weather this fall. I shared it out loud with a number of people, in person and on social media, "I'm looking forward to our Indian Summer in October." That was in September. Sure enough, we had a beautiful October in the Northland. The hiking trails were covered with orange energy, the smell of autumn and the leaves on the ground were indescribable, definitely my most favorite time of the year.

I rang the door bell to the left of the oversized white door that welcomed us as we climbed up the wide stairs. The front porch looked attractively untidy, with some dried maple leaves gathered around the feet of two white rocking chairs, standing to the left of the door. I patiently acquainted myself with the porch, and everything else that was on it. I always love homes with a porch, it's so welcoming. It wraps its arms around you as you come, giving you a warm hug. I saw a set of round black garden table and chairs taking a space across from the rocking chairs. A thick stack of dried maple leaves gathered nicely on the wood floor around it, it was charming. I rang the door bell one more time as I pushed my nose closer to the front door. "Where do you think they are?" I murmured to my husband. "They knew we were coming, did you push the door bell hard enough?" he questioned me. Just as I brought my hand up to the door bell for a third ring, I saw someone walk toward the door. "Hello, welcome," a cheerful greeting accompanied a big smile as she swung the door open, "Come in. Come in. No need to take off your shoes." I quickly danced my eyes around the foyer and up to the ceiling. "What a lovely home," I said, "I can't wait to see the rest of it."

We exchanged some small talk about our trip down, then she asked what time we wanted breakfast to be served the next day and if there was any dietary restrictions. My husband is on a see-food diet so he happily made the aah and uum sounds as the inn-keeper ran through the list of breakfast options. She then called out to her husband to help us bring our luggage up to the room. What a charming 109 years old home, I kept saying to myself as we walked up the stairs to our room. I immediately knew I would enjoy our next four nights here. "Good choice," I said to my husband. The bedroom was as charming with a fire-place, a king-size bed angled diagonally, lovely window dressing and cozy couch in the corner. I went straight to the bathroom, quickly turned around and got out of it with a smile. "How is it?" I heard my husband's voice as he was taking off his shoes. "Cute, and clean," I responded as I took off my coat. "Oh, I'm glad it passed the inspection," he teased me.

I'm particular about bathrooms, I think most people are es-pecially when traveling or using communal bathrooms. My husband's response though, in relation to the word *inspection*, is because of my more-than-dictionary definition of cleanliness. Even in our own home he considers my demand of cleanliness is beyond normal; I'm germophobic, he says. I, of course, dis-agree. Our home isn't spotlessly clean. I don't carry hand sanitizer in my purse or constantly wash my hands. I only do when I get inside the house from any activity outside, regard-less what activity that is, and before I eat. I do though, almost never touch any public door handles with bare hands, I use paper towel or napkin that I always carry in my pocket. You, my readers, be the judge of this.

That's the reason why I usually take control of and organize our traveling plan. I want to make sure things flow accordingly and nothing will bug me along the way – literally and figur-atively. But not today, not this trip, even though I couldn't resist checking the bathroom situation just now, as soon as we got in the room.

FINDING JOSEPHINE, FINDING ME

Charlie, my husband, had intended to be on this trip to Pittsburg, Kansas, since late summer. He wanted to find out where his paternal great grandmother, Josephine, was buried. He's been into family history for a long time now, he's the keeper of the family's old photos, boxes of them. Added to the treasures are some maps, postcards and books he bought through Ebay, flea markets, antique stores and auctions; things that are related to places where members of the family first resided after they emigrated from Europe, and where they moved around afterward. He has also accumulated many news-paper clips off the internet as a result of his research. One day, I caught him spitting into a glass tube and then dropped the tube in a cushioned envelope. "What in the world are you doing?" I asked him. Smilingly, he said "finding out my roots." He mailed his spit to the genealogy center in Utah to make sure he came from the ethnicity he believes he belongs to. How fortunate those people are who have access to such luxury in life – to be able to research their ancestors online, dig deeper through articles published in newspapers, get more information through genealogy centers around the country, or records kept at a court house. I know I won't be able to find out more about my ancestors, there are no records kept in my home country other than by family members -- in their minds and memories. I envy my husband.

Through many nights of research over the years, he found out that someone in his line of ancestry was related to a signer of the Declaration of Independence. Another one was the originator of the game Monopoly. He's fascinated with finding out about his roots. There are stacks of printouts lying by the side of the couch in our living room – obituaries, stories about members of the family that made it to the press. Before we went on this trip, he's promised me he would tidy up and file away years of research results accordingly. It'd be his winter project, he said.

In the past, promises like this would easily aggravate me. I would make sure he knew he had a promise he hadn't kept every time I saw the evidence was still there next to the couch. I would often nag him especially when I was overstressed, wasn't feeling accomplished and still had a lot to do around the house while he kept printing more articles, watching television, or doing things that were not productive according to my standard. Interestingly enough, this aggravating evidence seemed to know when to show up. It was whenever I was looking for things to nag on, to take my frustration out on. Otherwise, it was tucked nicely away somewhere in the back of my mind. I wonder why we can easily blow up over simple and trivial things, especially with those who are close to us.

I was still pleasantly surprised at how easy this trip had been; it was nothing about the drive or the traffic, it was about how I felt and responded to it all. To Charlie I was known to be uptight at times. "No, I'm not," would be my usual reaction when he tried to remind me not to be, of course with an uptight tone. I would never agree to it and was reluctant to admit it. This Pittsburg trip was our first long vacation together in a long time now that I thought of it. This would be our two-week road trip through Thanksgiving holiday and beyond. The last time we had a two-week-plus vacation was when we had our furniture business. Then, we would travel to Indonesia, my home country, once or twice a year for about three weeks each stretch. I remember those trips. I would have a rigid daily schedule to follow because of suppliers to meet based on the cities and areas we visited. Traffic had always been our biggest challenge so we needed to plan our moves to be efficient and productive.

Charlie had been to Indonesia many times but he wasn't as familiar with the areas so I always took control to arrange and plan the travel. We would be at breakfast by seven o'clock, hit the road and back at the hotel after the sun was down. The rigid schedule was needed because we also combined these trips with time for family and friends. We had fun, don't take me wrong, but it could have been more pleasurable if I wasn't as rigid and uptight. I realize it now. Charlie never complained about it but I remember him saying, "Can we get up later on weekends, and meet fewer suppliers?" Silence followed because I didn't immediately answer. "Maybe?" he continued. I can still hear the way he said the word *maybe*, with a tone that indicated it was alright if we shouldn't. Poor man, was I that strict a person? It sounded torturing to me as I now reflect back to that moment. I was brought up in a Catholic family and sent to Catholic school from kindergarten all the way to high school. I could picture the nun when I was in middle school, who checked our uniform as she made the round every Monday morning before we entered the class, a wooden ruler in hand. She would rip the hem off our skirts if she knew it was too short. I must have been like a Catholic nun to my husband, I'm embarrassed for myself just reminiscing.

Four years ago, we talked about taking a road trip for our anniversary. I had shared with Charlie I would love to see the forty-eight states by car. I had done enough traveling by air in my life. When we had our furniture business, we were traveling to a number of markets twice a year, dragging a trailer with a load full of products to showcase. I was enthralled by the naturally beautiful country side, the transition from farms to highways and sky-rising buildings, the people we met along the way. I wanted to see more of it because that's the America I wanted to explore. When the conversation about a road trip came about, Charlie mentioned we should look at going west to visit my sister-in-law who summers in Washington state with her husband. I had never been to that part of the country, "Yes, that would be fun. Where should we stop in between?" I asked him. Charlie drags and extends the word *well* when he's thinking or he's not sure about whether his answer will satisfy me, just like the way he said *maybe* before. And he did just that with this one too. "Weelll ... we can stop in Detroit Lakes?" he ended his sentence with a tone of unsure question mark. "What's in Detroit Lakes?" I asked again. I knew my mother-in-law grew up there, some more family history he might want to explore. "We could visit some family graveyards?" Again, his sentence ended with an unsure question mark. I wasn't sure how he would consider this trip a romantic one. "Celebrating an anniversary visiting dead relatives, huh?" I tried to make sure he knew what he was suggesting. He laughed. Suffice it to say, we didn't go on a road trip that year.

Here we were now in Pittsburg, looking for dead relatives and visiting others who had been six feet under probably for more than a century. I'd been embracing this trip so far. Instead of me doing the planning, I left it to Charlie to plan and arrange it. I knew how important this was for him. He'd been curious about where Josephine's final resting place was for a few years now. In fact, he took the initiative to search for a non-hotel place to stay, found the B&B online, made a reservation a few days earlier.

The first thing we wanted to do was to visit the genealogy center, which was in the Pittsburg Public Library. From the innkeeper we found out the library was within walking distance of the B&B. "Oh, let's walk," I immediately suggested to Charlie. I could record some steps into my Fitbit; a tracker that measures steps taken, and combines it with user data to calculate distance walked, calories burned, floors climbed, activity duration and intensity – that would make up for the eleven hours sitting in the car yesterday. As we were waiting for breakfast to be served, Charlie reminded me, "If we get there by ten, we'll have three hours until the library closes at one p.m. on a Friday. Do you have something to do while waiting?" I nodded several times, "I have my school module to listen to." I'd been back in school for the past four months, studying integrative nutrition, and loving it.

The inn-keeper came out of the kitchen with a banana parfait; a piece of banana, a dollop of Greek yogurt with fresh raspberries, blueberries and walnuts on top, nicely presented in an oblong bowl. After she vanished into the kitchen, Charlie started digging into it with a smile, he loves raspberries. I ate slowly, chewed well, remembering what I had learned from my school lecture. I was also reminded of my maternal grandmother's pearl of wisdom. She would say, "Chew thirty-two times before you swallow the food." I'm not sure where the number thirty-two came from. She would then say, "Don't eat like you haven't eaten for days, it's not lady-like." She believed you could know someone from the way one ate, talked, and walked.

As we were having breakfast and visiting with the inn-keeper, Charlie shared an interesting fact he had found out about the neighborhood. When he did some research about the family after he had found the B&B for us to stay, he found out that one of Josephine's sisters had lived across the street with her family, and Josephine's mother had lived there with this sister for a period of time. "Do you know the people from across the street well?' Charlie asked her. "Of course," she answered, "Well, they're quite into the family history as well, do you want to meet with them?" she continued. That was our intention when we found out about where we were staying. "I'll see what I can do," the inn-keeper says, and off she went back to the kitchen.

I finished my last bite when she came back with an egg and ham soufflé in a small ramekin. "Oh, my," I silently whispered, I thought the banana parfait was it, that was breakfast for me. I now had to eat even slower to make sure I'd enjoy and appreciate her effort waking up early to prepare this food. I loved the soufflé. Then, just as Charlie spooned up the last bite of his, she came back with yet another plate. It was a bunch of grapes. Now I had to say it louder, nicely of course. "Oh my God, this is a feast, thank you very much. You must have been busy in the kitchen very early." She noticed I already had enough so she offered to Ziploc the fruit for us to nibble on later. I agreed. Besides, I preferred to have fruit before anything else at breakfast, another one of my grandmother's pearls of wisdom. I was now more determined to walk to the library.

It was a nice short walk to the library, it was lightly drizzling. Luckily the inn-keeper loaned us her umbrella even though Charlie was reluctant to accept it, he didn't think we needed it. Besides, "It's just fresh water from the sky," he said, "and I'd rather hold your hand." So we did, and I used the umbrella too. The library was peaceful. Charlie was busy working with the librarian to find out in which cemetery Josephine might be. I was flip-flopping between listening to the school module through a tablet, ear buds in my ear, and jotting down some notes for this book as ideas showed up. I was enjoying my time, and enjoying what I was learning so far. Once in while I chuckled hearing some funny examples the teachers shared with us. I moved on to reading a nutrition book I brought with me when I was done with the school module. I kept the ear buds in to block the sound of the conversations I heard in the background.

This waiting game used to bug me, I didn't like waiting for others while I wasn't busy doing something. Reading wasn't considered busy enough an activity for me. I usually couldn't enjoy reading knowing I was waiting for somebody or something, I couldn't focus on it, flipping or browsing through a magazine, I could. I read books because I wanted to, not to kill time because I was waiting. Interestingly, not today. I was enjoying my time. It was peaceful, and ideas popped into my head every now and then. It was pleasantly surprising for me to realize how well I had responded to this trip so far, no fuss. I suddenly remember my brother's remark a long time ago, about me. "She has to be physically busy to feel productive." Was I that uptight a person?

Later, I asked Charlie to confirm whether or not he was familiar with a Type-A personality. He was, and he thought I am. I then googled Type-A personality to make sure I had the signs of one. Deep down, I wanted to be something else. I came across an article in the Huffington Post about it, which was posted a year earlier, regarding sixteen signs of a true or almost true Type-A personality. Twelve of those described me quite accurately – I'd like to say the old me. And they are:

1. Waiting in long lines kills you a little bit inside.
2. You've been described as a perfectionist, overachiever, workaholic or all of the above.
3. You have a serious phobia of wasting time.
4. You're highly conscientious.
5. You frequently talk over and interrupt people.
6. People can't keep up with you -- in conversation or on the sidewalk.
7. You put more energy into your career than your relationships.

8. Relaxing can be hard work for you.
9. You have a low tolerance for incompetence.
10. You'd be lost without your to-do list.
11. At work, everything is urgent.
12. You're sensitive to stress.[1]

"Oh yeah, you can be uptight at times," Charlie said. But the words *at times* actually made me feel relieved because that meant it wasn't always. "Really?" I couldn't believe what I just heard; didn't he see the difference in me just in the past two days?" I thought quietly to myself. "Once a Type-A stays a Type-A," was his response when I argued. "When do you think you can give up control, Sweetie?" he laughed, then immediately added, "Maybe a little softer on the edges now." He knew me well, controlling was the sign most people associated me with in the past. Darn it!

As far as I can remember, I have always been in control of my life. It went back as far as my younger years. When my dad started giving my brother and me pocket money to buy things we needed, I was in fourth grade. I started making a list of what I spent my money on; daily expenses were recorded to the cents then totaled at the end of the year. I felt accomplished knowing how much I spent annually and on what. The list making expanded into the trips I made, places I visited, movies I watched, then later in life also covered my career growth, the salary increment I received, awards I won. I, in fact, kept significant letters I received. I actually still have them in boxes in storage. I plan to make a scrapbook with them. This next one is quite embarrassing to admit, I also had a list of my period every month; when it started, ended and the total days, from the first time I had it until the day I reached my menopause. This list was actually a useful history to refer to when I had to undergo a surgery at thirty-one. You never know when you need a historical record. That was one reason I was obsessed with lists, I also felt accomplished and prepared knowing what I did. I was in control of my life. The number of lists was reduced tremendously when I moved to this country. I'm not sure why, but somebody will soon give me some credit for letting go of some control. I know that time will come.

We left the library a little after noon, it was still raining, and apparently the librarian had to volunteer at a different library on Fridays. Charlie got enough information he needed; the cemetery where Josephine's and her parents' burial spots would be, the address of another cemetery where there were more relatives buried, information about their farms, obituary notices and a few other things. We walked out of the library debating what to do next. Pittsburg seemed deserted at 12:30 p.m. on a Friday, and we were in the business area of town. "This will be fun," I said to my husband, genuinely. I was not trying to be sarcastic, as I might have been in the past. We weren't too hungry yet after a big breakfast so we decided to explore some antique stores in the area. I didn't know Kansas was known as the antique-store state. From a map we picked up by the library's door earlier that was what I gathered. The map showed the many stores we could find across the state, *State-side Antique Store Tour* was written on it, in big letters.

We spent more than an hour in one interesting antique store, beautiful items were displayed on two floors, and we visited with the owner. I was again surprised as I walked through each floor in the store; looking, reading, even counting parts of the many China sets that were displayed, noticing the ones I found interesting design-wise. I was never into antique store as much, Charlie is. He's giddy about antique stores, flea markets and auction places. I'm anxious every time he goes to an auction fearing what he will bring home. I went on a few auctions with him a few times, as anticipated I didn't have the patience to wait for the things he was interested in to come up. Sometimes, I found some items I liked and would go home and let him bid on them for me. Today, we had spent more than an hour in one antique store. That was quite an achievement, I was impressed I had the patience. Was I really that uptight before?

We were then heading toward Harry's Café just a block and a half away from the antique store. Rumor has it, Harry's has a reputation for serving some of the best pie in Southeast Kansas. We shared a piece of pumpkin and a piece of coconut pie. The café was like a scene from *Back to the Future*. A row of Formica-top tables lined up all the way down the length of the wall, booths wrapped around the middle area and on the opposite wall was a long bar counter stretching down from the front door all the way to the kitchen. This is a family café that's now run by a fourth generation. Our inn-keeper knows the owner. This morning she actually mentioned two cafes we could opt to go for breakfast while we were here. Harry's Café was one of them. We took our time, slowly enjoying our pies, tea and coffee while going through the information about ancestors we had gathered so far. The plan for the next day was to go to the cemetery where Josephine is, then explore the family farmlands and some more antiquing along the way.

We hit one flea market after Harry's, another hour is spent, Charlie was looking for some old postcards of Pittsburg but he couldn't find any. He was puzzled. In Duluth we can easily find many old postcards at flea markets or auctions. We walked back to the B&B through quiet, brick-street neighborhoods. We saw some houses were left empty and abandoned in between nice houses. After the economic down turn a few years ago, this former coal mine town had apparently never been the same, that was what we heard from a few people along the way today.

We got back to our room, stretched our legs. "There's a six-screen movie theater in town," Charlie said. "What's playing?" I asked, and he ran through the list. Some of them were movies we wanted to see before we left Duluth but didn't get to. Realizing how slow my response was, he immediately said, "We can think about it for tomorrow." In the past, I would agree to this proposal especially when it was only a little bit after five o'clock in the afternoon. The day was still long and we were on vacation, we would need to explore more and do more. I knew that was why Charlie suggested it. He might be worried I would be bored before the evening arrived.

Today, I somehow just wanted to continue enjoying the low-key afternoon. It'd been a pleasant time so far, I wanted to embrace what we had gathered – the breakfast and visit with the inn-keeper, the information we collected of the relatives, the places we went as we cruised around town, the people we met, the walk home, the neighborhoods, the many things I had been able to absorb. I was still pleasantly surprised at how much I embraced the experience of the last two days.

LOST AND FOUND

We were heading to the cemetery to find Josephine. Today's breakfast was as elaborate as yesterday's; mixed pineapple, cantaloupe and grapes, then pancakes, and cranberry scones. I opted to Ziploc my scone to go. Pittsburg wasn't as gloomy as the day before. As we were entering the cemetery, I asked Charlie, "Do you know where her spot is?" "Not exactly, but I have an idea based on the map," he answered me. "Here's a suggestion," he continued, "why don't you stay in the car, read or listen to your school module. I'll walk around and when I find Josephine I'll call you, so you don't need to walk around with me." "Oh, that's a great idea," I responded. He stopped the car on the right side of the main cemetery drive, halfway into it, and then opened the door and stepped out, "My God, what are you doing here? What a coincidence?" I heard him yell cheerfully. I immediately turned my head to the left and saw the tombstone. There it was, straight across the street in front of the opened car door, Josephine's burial spot. Her name was printed in big letters on the tombstone. "She knew you had been looking for her," I said in disbelief. I looked down at my hands, goose bumps.

The law of attraction only works when we're in action. He had been searching for her these past two years. It started when he was puzzled about the fact that his great grandfather Bill, Josephine's husband, was buried in Calvary Cemetery in Duluth, Minnesota, our home town. Bill did remarry after Josephine died, and his second wife was buried in Duluth as well. Josephine died in Duluth but we couldn't find the burial spot. Calvary didn't have a record of her being buried there. Where could Josephine be? Charlie started a mission to find her. He went to the court house in Duluth and found out through her death certificate that she was brought to another cemetery in Duluth, Forest Hill, after she died in January of 1899. After many visits to the cemetery, the caretaker later mentioned a record that showed Josephine was taken in May of 1899. People who died in the winter in those days were usually not interred immediately because of the frozen ground. It's common for the northern Minnesota's weather even now.

We approached her tombstone, took some pictures and then Charlie stepped back and saw two burial markers next to each other, off to the left of Josephine's. A male name on each of them, both only lived for a year, poor babies. Charlie then speculated that these might be Josephine's young sons. He remembered reading her obituary which mentioned that she had four children, but later, in all the articles he read about the family, he didn't remember reading anything about them except for the two daughters they had raised. The sons must have died young. These could be them.

Charlie was relieved. He finally found Josephine's final resting place and a couple of markers that might belong to Josephine's two young sons. I was happy for him. This trip had been worth taking. I was also pleasantly surprised to have found something else I didn't know had been missing. It was me. I've found me. This trip had opened my eyes to the fact that I was now a different person. A few of the twelve signs of a Type-A personality didn't exist on this trip; I had relinquished some control, I was more patient, waiting didn't seem to be an issue anymore. I, in fact, was more inquisitive, asking questions to find out more about Pittsburg and its people, and attentively listening to the answers. I noticed a few times Charlie gave me a signal to cut if off and get moving.

It certainly was an interesting revelation. I was amazed to realize that something right had happened. I felt I have re-awaken to life. There was a story behind each thing I saw, beauty in each person I crossed path with, some insights from each experience I just passed. This was the first trip in a long time when I realized how much in life I could still explore and embrace. I had taken time to stop, many times, *to smell the roses*. I was taking a deep inhale of gratitude. A journey I started had led me back to me.

Charlie suggested that I go back to the car. He said he wanted to clean up the little burial markers and straighten the grass edges around them. And then he wanted to explore the cemetery a little more, finding Josephine's parents and in-laws.

"I'll call you when I find them," he said.

As I was walking back to the car, my memory traveled back to a time of my childhood. It had been awhile since the last time I thought about it.

ೞೞ

"Not I,
or anyone else
can travel that road for you.
You must travel it by yourself.
It is not far.
It is within reach.
Perhaps you have been on it
since you were born,
and did not know.
Perhaps it is everywhere
- on water and land."

Walt Whitman
Leaves of Grass

ೞೞ

MY JOURNEY: FROM THE TROPICS OF BORNEO TO TROPICAL MINNESOTA

It was Sunday afternoon. We had yet to experience a sunny Pittsburg. The inn-keeper was so apologetic this morning, "I'm so sorry Pittsburg weather hasn't been friendly to you. It's expected to be drizzling again, on and off, today." She suggested that we hang on to her umbrella. The weather didn't bother us a bit. We were used to this kind of weather in Duluth, this time of the year. After driving through the areas where we suspected the family farmlands were, Charlie and I decided to go antique-store hopping -- lovely little stores we visited. Somehow, the gloomy and drizzly weather made an afternoon rendezvous with antiques seem suited. As I moved my feet slowly through the alleys of old treasures, I heard Nat King Cole softly serenading us in the background, *Embraceable You* -- one of my dad's favorite tunes I remembered hearing when I was a little girl.

I came screaming cheerfully into this world on a Sunday

morning, five minutes after five. My parents welcomed me with joy and love. Children arrive on earth pure and innocent, curious and ready to explore what lies ahead. Unfortunately, no one can predict what they may experience through their lives. There are happy, victorious, challenging, and painful moments their paths will cross. It's a mystery how their little mind processes each encounter, and how each will later manifest in different layers of life.

FIRST STOP: HIT BY LIFE'S STORM

I was born on the island of Borneo, one of 18,000+ islands that make up the country of Indonesia. My mom died when I was short of six years old, two days after she introduced my youngest brother to the world. The year was 1964. I remember being picked up by one of my distant relatives from school, somehow I can't remember who he was anymore, his face seems blurry now. I was excited to get off school early. I can't recall what subject we were on at that time. I was in first grade.

I noticed the car was heading somewhere, not the usual route home. This relative later said that he would take me to the hospital. Again, I was excited I had left school early and would see my baby brother. "What a privilege to be a big sister," I thought. The next scenes after that have been erased from my memory. I can't recall what happened at the hospital; whether I saw my mom, my baby brother, and how I got home. My memory bank picked up a scene, at home, when I walked into the wide busy living room of our house. Mom was lying on a long table to the right of the front door, covered with white sheet, quiet and still. The table seemed too high for me to see what she was doing up there. I couldn't see her full face, only her left cheek. I did notice, though, her tummy was as big as if my baby brother was still in it. I remember the times she let me put my ear close to it, picking up on the activity of the baby inside mom's tummy. And then I saw my dad talk to a few people around the coffin that was on the stands next to where mom was placed. Buckets and a long hose were brought in. And then dad asked me to leave the living room so I turned around and went the opposite way. As I was leaving the room I saw the beginning of a scene when dad was pumping mom's tummy, brown colored liquid running fast into the bucket through the hose that was inserted into her nose.

Later in life when I was in my teens, my aunt told me I was the usual cheerful kid that day. I rode my tricycle around the house going up and down the long hallway. The reason her stomach needed to be pumped was because she wouldn't have fit into the coffin. My baby brother's placenta didn't leave the uterus early enough, it burst and caused infection and her lungs were later drowned in volume of liquid. The only moment I cried, my aunt said, was a couple of days later when we left church after the funeral service. The coffin was closed and some people walked away with it. I asked dad, "She's not coming home with us?" He shook his head and I realized then I wouldn't see her again, ever. I didn't comprehend what death was. Later, I did.

I still remember that moment. I can picture the church, where we sat, how I turned my head following the coffin as they walked it out of the church. My older brother sat to my left and dad was on my right. It's still vivid in my mind. As time went by, that particular moment sometimes reappeared when I would see a six-year-old. A thought would come to me *that's how young I was when my mom died,* even though the emotion around it isn't saddening anymore. I don't intend for it to appear, it just does.

Recently, I was in New York City for an aunt's funeral. As I was visiting with my cousin who has three young children; nine-year-old twins and a six-year-old, I realized we suddenly talked about how he should later explain when his children asked about grandma's passing in more detail. My cousin and his wife had explained to their children in a way they thought was age appropriate, "Grandma is now with Jesus, we won't see her anymore but we can always remember her and the things we did together. Grandma will always live, in our minds." The children seemed to accept it. At that time, my moment re-appeared as I was looking at his youngest daughter, that's how young I was when my mother passed on. I was little.

My brother is two years older than I. I always look up to him not only because he's older but he seems to be more grounded and in control of his emotions. Our relatives recalled he was closer to our mom while I was to our dad. I don't remember seeing him crying after mom died, we never talked about our grief, we were too young to know what to talk about. And even as we were growing up, we never talked about it, so I never knew how he dealt with the loss. Family mentioned that he withdrew and became more quiet. My brother has never been an outspoken person, not then or now.

The nights following mom's passing, I would lie in bed before sleeping and construct a movie, in my mind, of our complete family; mom and all -- what we did, where we went, what we experienced as a family -- to avoid being sad. I played a different movie every night as I planned the life I would enjoy living. Over time, the movie I played in my mind varied depending on what I had to do the next day, school tasks I had to accomplish, the vacation we were embarking upon. The scenes got more vivid and intense when it involved things I had never done before, people I never met, bigger tasks to accomplish or new experience to face; like a final exam, school performance, and so on. The movie playing became a way of having mental rehearsals to calm myself down, as I was anticipating the unknown without a mother. A way for me to be mentally, and most probably emotionally, prepared for the things that came my way. A way to try to control the outcome and have it according to my favor.

IN TRANSIT: FROM CHILDHOOD TO ADOLESCENCE

Almost two years after my mom passed, my brother and I moved to another city and lived with my second oldest aunt, a widow with a daughter fifteen years my senior. The reason we had to move, as far as I could remember, was for better education. Surabaya is the second largest city in Indonesia on the island of Java, the most populated island in Indonesia. Dad didn't move with us, he had a business to run in our home town, but he would come and visit us as often as he could. It only took an hour and a half to travel between the two cities by airplane. I was excited to become a part of a new city even though I had to adjust to a new school, new friends, bigger class, and new language. Indonesia is an archipelago with thousands of islands, hundreds of ethnic groups and each has its own sub-language. Our native language is Indonesian, but the everyday dialect we hear outside of the formal setting will be the one of the state, or province as we call it. The home state where I was born has a dialect that's totally different from where I moved.

A change of place surely helped me focus on new things. I adapted to my new surrounding relatively smoothly. I don't remember any incident where my aunt or dad had to come to school because I, or my brother, did something that needed parents' attention. I still played the bedtime movie, it kept coming up with new releases and evolved accordingly as I moved onward and upward in school and life. It had become some kind of bedtime meditation for me, it soothed my mind. I fell into deep sleep and almost never remember dreaming. I slowly developed a passion for writing as well. It started with a journal, stories about the trips I had with my dad and brother. This passion was the seed that later turned into a career in advertising.

My life in this new city became more organized and planned. I liked the routine of walking to and from school with my brother. We revisited the route again later in life. It was quite a walk for a seven and nine-year old to take daily, round-trip -- country side, dirt roads, cutting through grass and bushes. We never recalled anything bad happening, the walks were filled by stories about friends, school and some jokes – what a simple and enjoyable life. Our schools were next to each other, mine was an all-girl Catholic school, and his was an all-boy one. Both of us completed our elementary years in our respective schools. My brother loved soccer. He developed affection toward the sport because the Catholic brother who ran his school loved it and coached the students. I remember waiting for him to finish his after-school sport by doing my homework in his classroom.

I was into performance. I loved singing, and was in a school choir. I loved dancing; I choreographed a dance and led a dancing group for a school performance. I won the first-place trophy for a Batik fashion show when I was in fifth grade. I worked in partnership with a dressmaker and designed my own clothing. I did the same with the hairstylist, and selected the hairstyle that would go well with the clothing I was wearing. I conceptualized how I delivered my walk. It felt really great when I took home the first-place prize -- I had an idea, I executed it, and I won.

When I was in grade school, all schools in Indonesia had a

flag ceremony every Monday morning before school started; it was mandatory for all students to attend this ceremony. I was one of the regulars that led the school in singing the national anthem. I would stand on a stage in the middle of the school courtyard, students lined up neatly in groups according to their grades, their eyes on me and following my lead. I was like a conductor of an orchestra. Most activities I was involved with required creativity, discipline, and planning. I thrived on those.

My aunt, who we also referred to as Mam – short for Mammie, a Dutch variant for the word mother -- was a terrific person. I started using the word *terrific* to describe her later in life, when I understood her role and what she did for us, raising a nephew and niece like her own. From being an aunt she became our Mam. The choices she made in life were true reflections of her commitment to family, her determination to enhance the quality of her life, the people under her care, and a total faith in her Higher Power. Family, work, and God were the fabrics of her life.

Mam learned one of the greatest lessons in life early on. The year was 1943, World War II was raging on, the Japanese invaded Indonesia after the Dutch ended 350 years of occupation. Mam was twenty-four years old, and her only daughter was three months old, when her husband was taken by the Japanese soldiers and never seen again. She never knew what had happened to him. That day, Mam surrendered her fear and hope to her Higher Power. Slowly but surely she built a solid foundation of faith which she never let go of until the day she died, she prayed the rosary every day. As a single parent, she then moved in with her parents and continued to build herself through life. In about twenty-two years she would move to a bigger city, have a house built, raise four children; my brother and me, a son of her cousin, and her own daughter.

She also took in two single aunts and later her own parents. She never remarried. She had a couple of life-threatening sicknesses but she beat them, and finally bowed out about a month short of her ninety-third birthday. She was the last one to go of eight children. She was a conqueror of life. And to me, that was an accomplishment.

Life had programmed Mam into an organized and productively busy woman. She was determined to achieve what she always imagined her life to be, with so many people under her care, she had to. As far as I can remember, she was always busy. She did many things in her life to raise her daughter, support her family, and put food on the table; from helping her brother-in-law in the dried-fish business, to running a hair salon from home, brokering properties, and buying and selling diamonds. Her life was always surrounded by people. She was a mediator and a connector. Almost every person who had done business with her ended up becoming her friend. These people's children got to know her well, and some even called her Mam. When some of her friends passed from this life, their children continued to be her friends, and remained that way through the winter of her life until she surrendered to the Higher Power. To many, she was a trusted friend and a mother.

Her busyness took her away from home often. She never traveled far, but she spent most of her day going around town meeting people. As with many Asian family traditions, we were, and are, used to living with extended family in one big house. My brother and I never had to be alone at home even though Mam was busy, there were always family members around to make sure we were not alone and had food on the table when we got home from school. I truly considered my brother and me fortunate children.

Mam's quick thinking and practical mentality made her a

strict, straight-to-the-point and matter-of-fact person. She made it clear what our obligations were. I never needed to be reminded to study or do my homework. I took care of it, school went smoothly. I don't recall any moment when she had to sit down and help me with school projects. I had a tutor for a period of time, who came to the house twice a week to help me get a grip on certain subjects and do homework. I wasn't the smartest student in the class, but certainly was never a disappointment. I was in control of my life. I also don't recall being hugged or kissed by Mam. She was never a lovey-dovey kind of person. I remember a time when I was in middle school, and my best friend was an only child. I often played with her after school in her home so I got to know her parents well. Watching how close she was to her mom – getting a hug and a kiss when she got home from school – and how much she could confide in her, I thought, "It'd be really nice to have a mother around."

Because Mam was always on the go, I don't remember or can even picture her sitting down relaxing or watching television in those twelve years my brother and I lived with her. When she sat at the dining table, the television was on and we were watching it, she would have something else to do, possibly work-related. She was always doing something. I remember when Mam was in her late eighties and I went to visit her, she would watch television still while doing something – cutting vegetables, folding laundry, folding plastic shopping bags – there was always something to do.

My teenage years weren't smooth and rosy, but the little bumps during my adolescence were considered normal, as normal as any teenager had to go through during that time. Mam was strict, especially when it came to my social life. I had to answer many tough questions about it. One night, this interrogation style reached its peak. That was the time I couldn't wait to go to college to live a freer life. That night, she had waited for my brother and me to come home from a high school party, similar to a prom. My brother was a senior and I was a sophomore. We got home an hour later than promised, at midnight, driven home by my brother's best friend. Mam had often seen him hanging out with my brother in his room after school. It wasn't enough for her that we got home safely, driven by someone she knew, because she was waiting for an hour not knowing what had happened to us. This was a time when there was no cell phone or text messaging. Her home didn't even have a landline. We had to go to a relative's home next door if we wanted to use a phone. I understood her frustration.

I couldn't avoid losing a mother, moving to a bigger city a year afterward, separating from my dad, adjusting to new environment with different language from what I knew prior to that, going through my adolescence being raised in strict upbringing by an aunt. I adjusted to those life happenings along the way. Those were the roads I had to travel by myself. I became an independent person and I knew how to take control of my life. I understood how parts of this life of mine had become a foundation of who I am: the things that happened and how they affected me, how I was raised, and the circumstances I was raised in. They were the things my roots latched onto for support. I could see similarities in characteristics between Mam and me. I carried those characters over from my childhood and they were amplified during my time living with her.

FINAL CALL: PAYING THE PRICE FOR THE EXCESS BAGGAGE

After graduated high school, I moved to Jakarta, the capital of Indonesia, to go to college. My brother had moved there two years earlier. A year after that, Mam moved to Germany to be with her only daughter and grandson. She eventually lived there permanently. The attributes that helped me thrive as an independent young person continued to nurture me. A few months after a short stint at an unrelated job as a human-resources staff at an oil and gas company, I landed a job as a copywriter.

Advertising is a 24/7 job, our minds never stop churning ideas. When I just started, I was happy to be hired, to have a job, especially as a fresh graduate out of college. I worked hard to prove that my boss had hired the right person, someone who would do her best, work long hours if needed, show ownership of projects under my care, and deliver the work better than expected. Anyone would agree work helped me practice the knowledge I learned in school, taught me a great deal about myself; my potential, my possibilities, how I was as a team member, how I was as a leader of a team, how far I could go to achieve goals. My life was centered on work, eight to ten hours a day. I was happy about it. The more praise I received about my discipline, the harder I strove to do better.

List writing, discipline, and control found their breeding ground and turned into perfection. Advertising provided an outlet for me to implement perfection. I believed I became a good copywriter because of this attribute. Friction, though, would come into play when I worked with a partner, especially with someone who didn't carry the same attributes I valued as important. I worked with a few team partners over the earlier years of my career. Once, I asked my supervisor to pair me with somebody else because "my partner slows down the work progress," I defended my reason. People would agree that my ways were usually right, but uneasiness in teamwork appeared because of the way I imposed it. I was demanding and of course, controlling and impatient. I stood my ground when I knew I was right, no negotiation and no comprise. I was a person of principle. I took things seriously to the point that there was little room for humor. I wonder how I built a successful career as a writer, in a creative environment, when I was strict and rigid. It makes me even wonder now, if only I let go and loosened up then, how much more success could I have gained? That's a price I had to pay. It's a humbling realization to understand how I was then as a person.

Sleeping was often a challenge for me back then. To execute a project accordingly I had to bring work home, often times my frustration from work came along with it – deadlines drawing near, team partner slowing down the process, tough clients. Then I had to get an early start to beat the traffic in the morning. The cycle repeated itself day after day. Stress accumulated even though I didn't feel I was stressed. I accepted the reality as part of work to the point of feeling proud about it. That meant I was working, building a career, I had a job. It was a signature of the advertising industry to burn the midnight oil when there was a big presentation to deliver the next day. Working late with a group of people somehow created a sense of comradery. You could get addicted to it. I was part of the initiation process. I was one of them. I felt I could then call myself an advertising person after that. I knew newcomers into the industry felt that way, too.

In December 2013, a piece of news circulating within the advertising industry in Indonesia had reached me. This news even made it into the regional online publication of South China Morning Post. Its headline stated, **Advertising writer dies after '30-hour shift' at global agency in Indonesia.** "Stepfather refuses to lay blame, insisting the girl he raised was on the cusp of success. Critics are unhappy with employer's work arrangements."[2] It was saddening to read about, and not surprising,

1

nothing much has changed.

At one point, my father asked me, "Do you have to work long hours most of the time?" He sensed something wasn't right. My excuse was I waited for the traffic to ease off. Instead of getting caught in traffic and spending time in the car, I might as well do some work at the office. Jakarta was a city of approximately eight million people at that time. Half of those lived in the suburbs and would come into the city every day to work. My home was twenty miles from the office. It would take me roughly two hours to go to work. In the evening, it would take an hour to go home if I left work after eight. Otherwise, I would spend another two hours traveling if I left right at the end of business hours, at five p.m. Rather than getting trapped in traffic, I opted to stay longer at work, or go to the gym located in the building.

Thinking about Jakarta traffic has brought me back to that time when hours were unproductively spent on the road. Right there was one source of stress. Traffic congestion was common, it's much worse now. The roads were shared by cars, busses, mini busses, taxis, motorcycles. Each vehicle fought its way through traffic, most didn't respect street signs. Early in 2014, I went back to Jakarta for a month. I could empathize with what my brother had to still endure every day. He has a driver, yet it's only so much you can do in the car – reading, reading, and reading. Nowadays smart phones, tablets and the like, have eased the boredom quite a bit. But when I see frustrating posts on social media coming from Jakarta, I know they must be trapped in traffic.

Just consider the fact how morning stress affected someone like me starting my work day. I carried the bag of traffic frustration into work almost every day. Then piles of work stress were added as the day progressed – client's call, work deadlines, team meetings, idea generating. When we had to call on a client, we would again deal with the frustration of heavy traffic. Dealing with stress was the high price I had to pay while building my career. And when my controlling and perfectionist nature came into play, the stress was amplified, and the bag became heavier over time.

Five years after I started my career, I left for my sabbatical year in New York City. I was disillusioned. I was swinging between feeling that my career wasn't growing fast enough and I had to work harder, to feeling I had enslaved myself being out of the house fourteen hours a day, five days a week. I didn't get to enjoy the softness of my pillow. I had had it. I needed to step away and regroup. I was so ecstatic when I started my career doing what I enjoyed most, writing. But now, I felt tired and unappreciated.

I took some courses related to writing and arts from New York University and the School of Visual Arts. I enjoyed my time in the Big Apple, exploring and absorbing the city and its people. I developed wonderful friendships with a number of people that continue until now. I loved all the writing and speaking courses I took. They were fun. I don't remember any friction that might be caused by my being uptight, except for one comment I now remember was jokingly shared by a classmate. We were planning a performance for a public speaking class. We had a group meeting and one classmate dropped out when we had gone deeper unto the practice. The performance would be attended by students from other classes. It was quite a production. "What should we do with the role now?" we wondered. Every person in the group already had a role, finding another person to fill the role was almost impossible. Other groups wouldn't let go of their members and practice time was limited. I can't recall precisely what the discussion was, I know we were intensely trying different options, and one friend said, "It's challenging to accept something that doesn't go your way, isn't it?" That remark was directed at me. The devil was following me to New York City. Someone caught it in action. Whether the remark was shared jokingly or not, she sensed it. I was controlling.

Toward the end of my sabbatical year in New York City, a couple of friends from the previous advertising agency, lured me into joining them to open an agency. "We need a writer-based partner," they said. I finally joined them. I was approaching the second half of my career, running our own agency was definitely unlike working for one. The pressure and responsibilities were higher, and the work was more demanding. My work days were extended to six days a week especially in the first couple of years. We were not just producing creative work like we used to do; we were leading a team, managing the business and the clients. The stress was four times larger.

I often micro-managed the team I was supervising in an attempt to control the outcome as planned. If it didn't flow accordingly, I would become impatient and end up doing the job. It stressed me out physically because I stayed longer at work to monitor every detail of the work. Other times, I would move the work to someone who was productive and burden this person with more jobs. The work was not distributed equally. Additionally, the effect of micro-managing numbed some of my team. They were not proactive, they were waiting for instructions. More stress for me. The vicious cycle was in action around the clock. It was self-inflicted, I know. I could see why I had become more uptight.

I was the same around health. I mentioned earlier that the first advertising agency I worked for had a gym in the building. At lunch time, I would go up to the gym. If I missed it, at six o'clock I would join an aerobics' class. It just felt good to accomplish such a thing. Even my boss noticed how disciplined I was about this. I wasn't really into strict diet but I watched what I ate. Vegetables were always part of my meal. I could live eating salad every day. I also developed a rule around personal hygiene; washing my hands especially after I spent time outside of the house or the office, brushing my teeth after every meal, taking a shower twice a day, especially before I went to sleep. Indonesia is humid. It's just too sticky not taking a shower twice daily, and I couldn't sleep soundly without a shower before bed. I imposed strict rules upon myself. I liked it because I felt accomplished doing so. I hardly got sick compared to those who took health for granted, I thought. This controlling nature later followed me into my marriage.

My life was wrapped tighter around work and my career, but I did have fun. I can't stress this enough. I did have friends, great and wonderful people who are still my friends. We did a lot of things together. But I also realized that most of the time when we tried to unwind during or after work, we still talked about work. Sometimes, we got even more riled up talking about it, adding stress to a stressful life. I could see it clearly once I was totally out of that work. It was revealing.

When it came to de-stressing, I usually went to a movie. I loved going to the movies and enjoyed it much. I went to see a movie almost every weekend. It didn't bother me when I didn't have a friend to go with, or someone who would go to the same movie. I just went alone. Saturday was my day to pamper myself. I would go to my usual salon in the morning and had my hair massage and body scrub with traditional concoctions. I would also do foot reflexology. I never missed this Saturday routine unless I was out of town. That was my recipe for de-stressing my life. I felt it was important to take care of myself. I remember a friend asked me, "Aren't you bored doing the same thing every week?" Why should I be? I felt accomplished. I completed my weekly chores. That made me feel great. That was what I called me-time.

I also enjoyed traveling, by myself. I could explore areas I was interested in and never had to depend on others or someone else to go with me. I could go shopping in an area or in a store I liked without having to wait for someone who wanted to go elsewhere. I could choose a restaurant and the food I liked without having to eat something I enjoyed less. I could skip or push back meal time or do something else first. It's the freedom to do things my way when I wanted them. That was the freedom I treasured when traveling. This solo travel started because often times it was difficult to coordinate vacation with friends I enjoyed spending time with. There were always work-related issues that got in the way, or families. I learned not to depend on others a long time ago, so off I went on my own. It was liberating to be able to do things by myself. And I stuck with it.

This independence went deeper into my life. I became selective in my love relationship -- overly, some said, judgmental. Why not? I thought. This was my life. No one was going to come crawling in helping me if something happened to my relationship. If I had to be in one for the rest of my life, I needed to be selective. I needed to know I could live with the choice I made. That control freak was in action, again. I had a few serious relationships, but my tolerance reached its limit at a certain period of time. When I traced it back, they all seemed to be on its three-year mark. That was usually the time I would let go -- when I thought he wouldn't change or I couldn't tolerate this life I would live for the rest of my life.

I had a couple of broken hearts along the way, but the

decision was easy to take when I rationalized the facts that it was the right decision. The broken heart was not about some sadness losing someone I loved, but it was the regrets that I had wasted my time and life on someone who didn't share my values. That was what my close friends meant by being overly judgmental. I would argue with them and say, "It went both ways. He could have broken up with me if he thought I wasn't the right one for him; he had that right." "But when would that happen?" they argued back. "You were good enough for him; but he wasn't good enough for you. There may never be one out there."

I remember those discussions about love with close friends. I didn't want to hold on to someone or something if I didn't know what the end would be, if I couldn't control the outcome - - not knowing was torturing for me. I didn't want something I loved and enjoyed to be snatched from me. So, when things weren't as perfect as I could imagine it, I'd rather let it go then, instead of bearing the pain later. The chatter in my mind could get louder at times, "My mom was taken away from me when it was least expected, I didn't have control over it. I wouldn't repeat that feeling again. I would control when and how things happened."

One of my relationships almost reached the altar. It was the only relationship I had when my dad asked me whether it would move on to the next stage. "Just let me know when I should fly in and be with you," he said. I don't know whether he thought this relationship was different from the previous ones, or, whether he felt it was time for me because I was thirty. My then boyfriend and I had talked a little bit about marriage. We thought we could move on to the next stage in our relationship. Yet as soon as we talked about it, issues seemed to be surfacing. They showed up front and center, one by one, to remind me of my principle, "If you can't see yourself living with the choice you make for the rest of your life, you shouldn't do it." I went through a few discernment processes in my mind, weighing the pluses and minuses, the pros and cons. I dragged my feet to plan the wedding. I kept pushing back the proposal day. I didn't want our families to meet if I didn't know this would be the path I wanted. Otherwise, I would have to arrange and get them all back together again, in the same room, when the proposal had to be broken. I needed to be sure. For Indonesians, marriage proposals are done between families. It does start with a decision between the couple who are in a relationship, it will then be formalized by a meeting of the two sides of the family. That's when the male side officially proposes to the female's side.

I later found out dad had asked my brother what happened, why I hadn't confirmed the date and was stalling my decision. All that my brother said was, "This is her journey, she has to decide for herself on which path she travels. I know she won't make a decision she can't live with." My brother, who had been the only close family member who I was never separated from - - except for the two years he was already in college ahead of me -- knew me very well. He's the wise brother I admire and look up to. I couldn't blame anyone else if this was my decision. I would live with it and make it work. But to make the journey forward more enjoyable and worth taking, I had to think hard and weigh things well. I was right on this one, on all counts. All roads led back to validate a decision that we were not meant to be together, we were just two different people. It sounded cliché, but it was true.

When we finally broke up, my brother and I had a few discussions; some were among close friends of ours, about whether there was a certain pattern in my relationships, or in my life, I needed to note. I seemed to be attracting similar types of boyfriends whose characteristics I didn't get along well with. "You knew about it from the beginning, I'm sure," he said. He was right. I had a list of traits in a man I would consider to be the marrying type. Yes, a list of ten qualities I looked for in someone. Based on the relationships I had so far, none of them met the top five qualities on the list; the important ones to me, they were prominent. I must have known from the very beginning they didn't meet my criteria. How could I miss that?

I didn't miss it. I knew they didn't meet the criteria. But my thinking was, after a couple of unsuccessful experiences, I had to give relationship a chance. I either could help him change or I would, and accept him for what and who he was. But it was impossible to change someone, and it was almost as impossible to change myself. I know I'm not the one and only angel alive and available, but why would I be drawn to someone I knew, from the very beginning, wouldn't fit me? What attracted me to someone like that? The realization came long after that. It was the control, again. I wanted to fix someone who I loved on many counts, but had some defects. I believed I could change him. I could see the same pattern repeating itself. I considered someone like that as challenging, mysteriously attractive. I could mold him the way I wanted it, fix him, and create my future the way I envisioned it – control the outcome.

The boyfriends I was attracted to were generally the ones who didn't mind being fixed, being taken care of, they would gladly surrender to my rules – this is what to do, how to do it and if you can't do it, I will. I became the provider of everything. Some men tolerated that, the ones who didn't mind being controlled. Problems started creeping up when I felt over-whelmed. Things weren't taken care of or they weren't done right if I wasn't there to do it. A litany of whys started rushing through my head. Why should everything wait for me? Why couldn't he do it right? Why couldn't I rely on him? Why, and more why.

On the flip side, of course he wouldn't or couldn't do it right. I took care of things from the very beginning. He didn't know he should. Even if he could, he ended up not doing it right. So why bother? That was quite a revelation. Einstein, I believe was the one who said it best, "Insanity is doing the same thing over and over again expecting different results." But, attraction occurred unintentionally. I didn't plan it, it just happened. I was just drawn to someone who was mysteriously challenging; usually was a quiet or reserved type who appeared to be independent and strong, but vulnerable inside and hid it well.

Revelation is one thing, changing is another thing. It was challenging for me to change, controlling had become my second nature. It's embedded deeply into my being. The wedding that didn't happen made me even more stubborn. I stood tall to guard my principle. I'd rather not marry anyone if I had to compromise my values and the qualities. I stayed single for another thirteen years after that. I buried myself even deeper into my career. I continued to travel and go to the movies, alone. I had great friends who were also single and we, of course, compared notes that validated the reason we stayed single. There were times when I felt I should loosen my criteria and modify the qualities I was looking for. It was just difficult to find someone that perfect. Friends would joke about it, "Surrender now or die waiting." I thought about it for a while, but my belief system was so strong and rooted, it was challenging to let go.

At one point, I was thinking about having a child or adopting one. I felt my biological clock was ticking. Most of my friends had children by then, and those who stayed single were numbered. I consulted with a lawyer friend of mine and did some research on my own about artificial insemination. I then learned the challenges I would face as a single parent. Indonesian culture and marriage law considered children who were born outside of wedlock as illegitimate, and they would be declared as one on the birth certificate. And unfortunately, my friend said, the law didn't recognize artificial insemination as legitimate. My brother suggested that I step away and go on a spiritual retreat, to go within and ask myself the true reason I wanted to have a child. "Is this decision only for you, so you can experience being a mother? Or, do you include the child's life in the picture? You will need to dig deeper into your mind and heart for this decision." That was my wise brother talking. This was the one instance I didn't fight. I didn't try to control the future of another being I hadn't even met. That's the price I had to pay for being single. I let the idea go.

BOARDING THROUGH A NEW GATE

Deep into the second half of my career, I again found myself disillusioned. I wasn't sure advertising was the land I needed to keep plowing. I couldn't seem to harvest anything out of this dried land anymore. I needed to explore other ground, but I didn't know what, where, or when. I felt stranded in the intersection of life. I had been involved in this industry for so long, starting a new path seemed to be a daunting task. Through a colleague of mine, I learned about a self-discovery program she had taken a few months earlier. She was raving about it and thought I should check it out. It was an experiential program that helped people be in touch with their true purpose and possibly reach a breakthrough. "I can't explain it to you, you need to experience it yourself," she said. "What do I have to lose?" I thought.

48

It was a mind-opening program, to say the least. I realized I had been drifting through life for a long time and disconnecting with my true intention. When work becomes the center of your life, you will, over time, lose sight of your own goals, intention, and purpose in life. We are hired and compensated to help achieve someone else's goals, in most cases it's the company's. I understood that fully. In doing so, my own goals and my life's intention got pushed to the back burner, and slowly they were forgotten. This program, called AsiaWorks[3], had helped me reconnect with my personal goals, rekindle my dreams. It gave me fresh fuel to look at life from a different point of view and allow surprises to take their course. I thought it was a great idea to step aside, recharge my life's battery, and take inventory of which baggage from the past I needed to let go to ease my journey ahead.

As a result of AsiaWorks, I consciously made time for my dad and truly treasured a deeper love I had for him. Coincidentally, it was the last year of his life. This was a man who decisively stayed single for eleven years after his wife had passed -- the reason being, he would dedicate his attention to his children. He let them grow to be an adult before he looked for a partner for himself. My brother once told me, "When Pap remarries, it'll be to find a life partner for him, not a mother replacement for us." He was entitled to that. I had a rough time under-standing this idea at the beginning, because I became so close to him after my mom passed. Bringing in another person into our life was upsetting for me. I was a possessive and controlling being.

In addition, I opened up my time to do volunteer work for terminally sick children and their parents. I spent four hours a week with two young children of unfortunate families; reading books, playing with them, visiting and emotionally supporting their mothers. One of these children became very close to me. It was humbling to witness how a simple thing like reading a book could lighten up a child's day and in turn put a smile on a mother's face. He died on one evening before I was scheduled to come back. His mother called and told me, "He asked for you earlier today, and I told him you would come tomorrow," she said. He was four years old. I continued visiting with his mother over the phone periodically through the year. She was a sweet woman.

I then discussed my career options with my boss and he agreed to release me from the stressful and taxing daily work. He would give me a new area to explore, an area that would allow my best traits to expand – brand planning; to build and grow brands, to expand their possibilities to enrich the people that use them, and build stronger connections with them. It would have been an intellectually and creatively stimulating project to handle. And before I entered that career door, the Universe barged in, in a great way, and steered my life in a different direction.

These were life's simple, yet meaningful, goals I started with. I got in touch with values in life I had overlooked, and forgotten, for the past eighteen years of my career – family, community, rewarding work, and personal goal. I'm not saying a five-day AsiaWorks program could miraculously change someone's life. It takes two to tango – I needed to be ready, itchy to change and searching. I heard this phrase often quoted by many, "When the student is ready, the teacher will show up." I was ready. Instead of being stuck staring at a closed window, I now saw a new gate open. A year after I completed AsiaWorks, I met Charlie, who was vacationing with a friend in Bali – the island of the Gods.

The family, missing mom, on my First Communion.

Inge Maskun

ॐ

*"If you begin to understand
what you are
without trying to change it,
then what you are
undergoes a transformation."*

Jiddu Krishnamurti

ॐ

3

KEYS TO MY TRANSFORMATION: A JOURNEY
FROM HUMAN-DOING TO HUMAN-BEING

I landed in Duluth, a seaport city in the state of Minnesota, the land of 10,000 lakes, in spring of 2002. It was a thirty-three-hour journey crossing the Pacific Ocean with one overnight and a few transits. I had visited this city before, in the winter, but this was now a different season. I was welcomed by sunny and warm-at-heart weather, unusual for Duluth this time of year. I felt this city was wrapping me tight with its warm energy. The smell, the look, and the sound of the afternoon were different from what I was used to experiencing in Indonesia. I took in a long breath of fresh air as I stepped out of the airport with Charlie. It was crisp and fresh. He looked at me and said, "We are home." We arrived on the same afternoon as the one we had left behind on the other side of the world. It was just mind-boggling to realize we had experienced two afternoons on the same day, in two different places. I seemed to have stood still and the world turned 180 degrees around me.

Charlie's sister and her husband picked us up at the airport.

The car was curving out of the airport area when they suggested that we stop and take a picture in front of the Duluth Airport welcome sign. It was official, "I'm here, now I get to call this place home as well." As the car was gliding down Haines Road, I couldn't stop looking out the window and realizing I wasn't trapped among a gazillion vehicles on a congested Jakarta road. Suddenly, I could hear the stillness of the moment; trees moving back slowly, patches of snow hanging tight on the ground in the warm spring sun. I could see the surface of Lake Superior as we were winding down toward Skyline Boulevard. Something was missing. I didn't miss the traffic. I missed the life and the people in it. Tears were silently cascading to my heart, a separation I was ready to take, but still, my heart was tip-toeing between happy and sad. "Give it a time, it'll heal itself," I gave myself a pep-talk.

We spent a little bit of what was left from the unusual warm afternoon sipping tea. We cracked open the front window of the house to let the fresh air fill the room. The sun started to set. From a distance, I saw it blowing the deep orange kiss of the day, and then a goodbye slowly turned into a bright smile for the other side of the world. I remember the many long-distant phone conversations I had with Charlie when we were still dating, 9,000 miles apart. Most of them were happening while I was in the car on the way to work – a way to take a break from Jakarta's traffic. Once in while he would abruptly switch the conversation and say, "Are you looking at the sun?" Sometimes, when Jakarta high rises didn't block off my view, I would respond, "Yes. Yes." Then I would bring him back to our conversation. The first time he posed that question to me, I wasn't sure why he did it. He was as giddy as a child helping me realize we were looking at the same sun. It was signaling the end of the day for him, but a new day for me. There are twelve or thirteen hours separating Duluth and Jakarta, depending on daylight savings time. Duluth is always a half a day behind. Charlie used to be my yesterday, and I was his tomorrow.

KEY #1:
I CAN SEE CLEARLY NOW HALFWAY AROUND THE WORLD

Life in a new environment showered me with new spirit and energy. I was on a journey to explore this whole newness of life. My growing up wasn't as easy, there were some bumpy roads I had to go through, but who didn't? I felt fortunate to have the life I had. My family wasn't perfect, and the circumstances I was growing up in weren't ideal, but I consider my life a blessing: I had a family, a home, food on the table, the opportunity to enjoy school and learn, and later built a career. I had great memories of the trips I had with my dad and brother. I still treasure those memories and the chance to explore parts of our country and others. There were people who were less fortunate than I. I don't have any complaints.

I'm now welcomed into my husband's family with such generosity and love. Charlie is one of nine children; he's the middle child, was born and raised in Duluth. His family gatherings are always fun and loving, full of laughter and food. I never feel left out. I blended nicely into my new family from the very beginning. Watching Charlie's siblings relate to each other, brings back a warm memory of my growing up. My maternal grandparents and their eight children, plus a son from my grandfather's earlier marriage, fit in like a key to a padlock. My grandfather was a kind-hearted and loving man. He, and my grandmother, developed a ritual to have a family brunch on Sunday. It was always a big gathering with those who lived close to them. Our big, long dining table was covered with white linen, chairs were placed so tightly next to each other we would rub arms with those who sat next to us. It's déjà vu all over again. I feel like I never left home.

Charlie and I were dating for a little over a year before I finally moved forward and embarked on a new stage of life with him. One of my best friends was surprised to hear the news about my moving to a new country. She wondered whether I had given this decision a deeper thought, "This is so unlike you," she said. Unlike me because I usually exercised all possibilities, analyzed each step, dissected the plan and got all ducks in a row. "What got into you?" she must have thought. I, for one, was surprised at how smoothly everything fell into place. There was no hesitation or second-guessing. In fact, the way forward presented itself, I didn't look for it, I just moved onward accordingly. That's how I knew.

When I came back from my end-of-the-year vacation in Duluth, I mentioned to my boss that I had become engaged and would eventually move to the United States. I also shared with him I wasn't in a hurry, and there was no definite moving date picked out yet. He congratulated me and said he would start looking for my successor, and he found one within five weeks. First clue.

Then, one Sunday afternoon while watering my front garden, I shared the news with my next door neighbor, and she asked me what I planned to do with my house. "Have you listed it?" she asked me. "Not yet," I responded. I was still doing my research on who I wanted to work with, and when I was ready to do so. A few days after that short neighborly conversation, her brother-in-law made an appointment to see my house, then a couple of days later he told me over the phone, "I'll take it. You can live there as long as you want. I'm not in hurry to move in. The house I'm renting is still good for another year." Second clue.

The following weekend, I spent my Sunday with my brother and his family. We casually talked about plans and I mentioned how they had progressed in the last one month. He then looked at me and said, "What are you going to do with your car?" He knew my car was only four years young. "I'll sell it, of course," I said nonchalantly. "Well, then," he said, "We'll buy it. You can still use it until you have to go." My sister-in-law, apparently, was ready to trade in hers. Third clue.

How many more clues did I need? When those three important things had been spoken to, I was basically jobless, homeless and carless. A month after my conversation about the car with my brother, Charlie came back to Indonesia to pick me up. Two weeks after I landed in Duluth, our union was official according to the law, and a year afterward we had our church blessing. My brother walked me down the aisle. He came with his family and my Godmother from Indonesia, Mam and her daughter came from Germany. The last evening before Mam's departure, we had a chat in the bedroom, "I'm happy for you, you have found a husband, and a family who loves you. Now I don't need to worry anymore."

Mam had met Charlie more than a year prior to our wedding. We visited her in Germany, and Charlie asked Mam's permission for my hand. "He seems to have a kind heart," she said to me then. But Mam never met Charlie's family yet. I could hear her words, I was sure it was similar to the ones I used to hear when I was a teenager, "Whose kid is that you're friends with?" Whether they were male or female, she would ask the same question. No harm intended, it's just commonly inquisitive question any parent would ask their children then, and most probably now as well. As a guardian to my brother and me, she took her responsibility seriously.

One week after our engagement in Germany, while we

were traveling in Europe, my cousin – Mam's only daughter – called and gave me the news that doctors had found cancer in Mam's throat. "Further tests are needed to determine how serious this is," she said. I talked to Mam briefly. She was in her usual upbeat manner, and I could hear her positive mindset projected through the phone. I was never worried about her ability to conquer life's challenges. A month after that phone conversation, I called her again to see how she was doing, "I'm just fine. I eat well and sleep as well," she brushed away my concern. She was a tough cookie. She cooked, cleaned the apartment, did Qigong twice a week, and of course, prayed the rosary daily. Every time I spoke with her on the phone, she asked of my plan, "Keep me in the loop, I need to make plans ahead of time," she reminded me. It's my wedding she was after.

Many months later I found out the real story. At first, after further tests, the doctor decided not to pursue surgery. He didn't think cancer would grow as fast for an eighty-three-year-old. He also didn't want to take a risk of damaging her vocal cord. "We'll continue monitoring it closely and will take appropriate steps accordingly." That was what I had heard from my cousin. The next check up was scheduled in three months unless she needed immediate action sooner. Apparently, Mam made an agreement with the doctor. "My daughter is getting married in America. I have been waiting for this moment for a very long time. I have to be there," she said. The oncologist then said, "That's truly wonderful news. You focus on going to America, and we'll deal with the cancer."

When her three-month mark was up, an appointment was scheduled to see how the cancer was progressing. The procedure required her to stay overnight at the hospital. Two days prior to it, I spoke with her on the phone. "The cancer is gone," she said to me confidently.

"Mam, how do you know? Your procedure isn't until Tuesday," I was puzzled.

"I just know it," her voice overcame me, "I had a dream last night. The Blessed Mary showed up and touched my throat. I don't have it anymore."

"Oh, Mam," was all I could say. "Here it is again, Mam and her dreams," I thought to myself. She was a person who remembered her dreams, vividly, and to her they always had meaning. She was just a carbon-copy of her mother in this territory. I promised her I would call again in a few days to see how things went. She beat the heck out of cancer. It was gone, they couldn't find it. "Ha! Don't mess with my Mama," I told myself. Eight months after the verdict, she came to my wedding, and during that visit she conveyed what she witnessed to me. "I'm happy. I'm at peace knowing how lovingly your husband and his family treat you. I can go any time now." She enjoyed ten more years of her life after that.

Growing up, I remember hearing my folks talk about those who were dating our relatives, people who might become part of our family. My brother and I sometimes still joke about our grandmother's candid ability to read others, just by being with and watching them. Regardless whether it would be true or not, she could convincingly make us believe her instinctive mind. Now Mam shared her observation with me, "You know how a man will treat his future wife by watching how he treats his mother." Charlie passed the test. I could sense Mam's feeling of relief. Initially, she was worried, "You're too far away from our family," she said. Mam didn't speak English or understand what people said during her visit for our wedding. She watched and listened with her heart, and she knew.

I moved halfway around the world yet I don't feel alone, or

lonely. The daily pressure of everyday life went down tremendously; from working long hours and being trapped in traffic, I now enjoyed chores of opposite contrast. Cooking channels became my daily company. I turned into a diva in the kitchen and obsessed with cooking. All my life when I was in Indonesia, I never had the need to cook, for me or anyone else. This may sound unusual for many people in this part of the world, but most households in Indonesia's cities have a live-in cook. When I was little, my family lived in a big long house which was also shared by my maternal grandparents, the oldest aunt and her husband. For Indonesians, and most Asians, especially at that time, it was common for many family members to share the same house. My grandmother was the queen in the kitchen. She controlled and took care of what ended up on the table. When my brother and I moved in with Mam, she had a cook who had been working for her after she lost her husband. She became part of the family, and she was a wonderful cook.

I remember the time when Charlie and I were dating, I don't think he knew I was at the level of a kindergarten student in the area of cooking. The first time I visited Duluth, we were entertaining his family on Christmas Eve. I decided to serve Mam's Linden Soup -- pea soup; her signature dish, and my brother's favorite. A few days prior to Christmas Eve, I was frantically in a long distance communication with Mam, between Minnesota and Germany, to get the recipe right. The challenge started as I was trying to convert sizes and measurements. Mam's recipe is based on metrics and everything here is based on ounces and pounds. Here's the recipe she gave to me over the phone – green peas, potatoes, carrots, onion, green onion, garlic, chicken sausage and bacon, salt and pepper. Mam learned how to cook the old-school way, most probably from watching my grandmother. Everything is *kira-kira* -- in

Indonesian it means, just wing it.

I had been in the kitchen since two o'clock that Christmas Eve; cutting, chopping, preparing dessert and a salad to go with the soup. By five o'clock, the soup didn't show promising progress, it was still uncooked. I had Mam back on the phone, I couldn't figure out what went wrong. I ran through the steps, and we finally realized I didn't soak the peas overnight. No wonder they were stubborn! I had to scoop the peas, transfer them into a bowl and mash them. I managed to serve a delicious soup on my first attempt to entertain my future in-laws, but I almost peed my pants preparing it. It was chaotic. I wasn't going to repeat the same experience again. I needed to be great at cooking. I experimented diligently; cooked, baked, and then stretched it further, entertained. Charlie and I still enjoy many gatherings with friends and family in our home.

I became a domestic queen, a homemaker. And I was a good one too, much better than I used to be. Practice made perfect. I took advantage of the leisure time I had because I could only find work when my social security card had been issued. This was a well-deserved long vacation for me. I needed it. I also practiced driving on the opposite side of the road. it wasn't challenging because Duluth traffic was so friendly and forgiving. At an intersection with an all-way stop sign, I'd be chuckling watching how each car waited to give the other a right to move first. I was embarrassed to realize how much my people, Indonesians, had lost their manners on the roads in Jakarta.

I kept myself busy with home up-keeping; grocery shopping, cooking, cleaning, doing laundry, ironing, gardening — things I never had to do when I lived in Indonesia, hardly ever, except for grocery shopping. I was fortunate, I had a live-in house helper, as with many households in Indonesia's cities. I also volunteered to read with two title-one students; first and second-graders, twice a week. It was such a pleasant time I had with them. I got to familiarize myself with common books elementary students were exposed to. I must say, Amelia Bedelia's series was my most favorite one. What a wonderful way to learn figures of speech and not to take various terminology literally. I learned a lot from it since English wasn't my first language.

Duluth grows fast on me; its people, its dynamic roads of hills and valleys, its ocean-like Lake Superior, its fresh tap water, the serene trails just a few minutes away from wherever you are, its lovely summer and fall. Awfully nice. When I just moved to Duluth, I remember watching my husband easily go into a little chit-chat with people as we go around town; at the store, gas station, restaurant, and other public places. At first, I was surprised at how many people he knew. I understood this was a small city, "... come on, he couldn't have known that many people?!" After I witnessed a few instances, I started asking him, "Who was that you were talking with?" And most of the time he would answer, "I don't know," smilingly, with a questioning look on his face. I eventually accepted the fact that most Duluthians were just like that, you could strike a conversation with almost any one you just met. That's Minnesota Nice, they live up to that. I felt immediately at home, and became one. Three months after I called Duluth home, one of my very best friends, Ditta, visited me from Indonesia, and she was surprised, "I know this is a small city compared to Jakarta. But, come on, how many people have you known already?"

Six months after I moved to Duluth, a former client of mine invited me back to Indonesia for a quick trip as part of a five-person think tank team, brainstorming for product ideas. I was delighted to get a chance to go back. During those three weeks

I realized how much my mind had shifted, for the better, even from the standpoint of pollution and traffic. When the airplane was about to land in Jakarta, I could see a thick fog above the city. And as soon as I walked out of the airport, I was met by the smell of smoky air. I could feel it entering my system. And then a few minutes later, I was back on Jakarta's congested roads.

The last advertising company I worked for before I moved to Duluth was headquartered in Chicago. I remember a conversation I had with a friend from that office when he learned I was moving to Duluth. "Do you know where Duluth is? Have you experienced winter there? Have you been there?" I was bombarded by a chain of questions to make sure I knew what I might turn my life into. Calmly, I responded with a smile, "Yes. Yes. And Yes." He didn't seem to believe my response, "But you're such a city girl!"

Those questions did cross my mind when I was visiting Duluth the first time. I thought about it, "Will this be too small a city for me?" Duluth's population was around 86,000 people, not much has changed since. Greater Jakarta was around twelve million people when I left, it certainly felt it was doubled six months later when I came back. I was nervous driving in Jakarta. My brother had me use his car, with a driver, to get around. "The traffic have multiplied so much, and so fast?" I remember saying to him. "It's the same traffic, you're just not used to it anymore." My brother made me realize I had changed.

Living halfway around the world had helped me use the ample time I had to regroup and refocus. I didn't have that time before. I pushed myself too hard, not smart, at work. I was addicted to hanging out at work. It took crossing a deep Pacific ocean for me to see a wider horizon, the pollution in my head was then blown away, and the road ahead suddenly became clearer. I had options to explore, advertising wasn't the only way. The short trip back to Indonesia presented an avenue for Charlie and me to pursue something that can bring us back to Indonesia more regularly. Later that year, we launched a business importing one-of-a-kind home and garden furniture, as well as home accessories, from Indonesia.

KEY #2:

A FRUITFUL ENCOUNTER FOR THE BODY AND MIND

Five years into our import business, a potential wholesale customer I met at a market in Minneapolis asked me about the mangosteen[4] fruit. I never heard of the mangosteen before, but when she showed me the picture, I almost screamed with amazement, "Where did you find it? How did you know about it?" I was very curious because I knew this was a fruit typical to Southeast Asian countries. You couldn't grow it outside of the Tropics and couldn't find it in this country either. Unless, maybe, in a frozen form. Its place of origin is unknown but is believed to be the Sunda Islands and the Moluccas, which are in Indonesia. We call it *manggis* in Indonesia – juicy snow-white fruit, in segments, softly sweet on your mouth, wrapped in a dark maroon-purplish, thick and tough skin. It's no larger than a tangerine. It snuggles right into your palm like a ball.

I was right, the fruit wasn't available in North America. This customer enjoyed it in the form of a juice. An American-based company out of Utah was the first one that introduced this product into the market, using a network marketing distribution method. One of its founders came across the fruit when he worked in Southeast Asia. The customer asked me what I knew about the fruit. A floodgate was opened. My childhood memories came rushing back, watching my grandmother take advantage of the powerful benefit this small fruit had to offer when we were sick. We used it for many things: diarrhea, fever, burns, sprained ankle, skin problems. I also remember a time in our childhood when my brother or I had a loose tooth, we would keep wiggling it with our tongue until it fell off. Then we would bite the rind of the mangosteen, a small part of it, to stop the bleeding quicker. We also used it to die fabrics, the maroon-purplish color was just perfect to create a deep red color, even as a marker to do school projects.

One time, my grandmother was ill, we already lived in Surabaya at that time. I was too small to remember exactly what had happened, but I do remember seeing her change a compress that was attached to her lower back every afternoon. That compress was the mangosteen poultice that was made fresh on a daily basis. Our house helper would grind the dried rind of the fruit with a stone grinder and immediately apply it to my grandmother's lower back. I can't remember what other natural ingredients were added to it. I only knew my grandmother was back to walking after that, her usual self. The use of herbs and plants for healing purposes has been a part of our family, and most Indonesians. It's folk medicine – *jamu*, we call it; no scientific evidence needed, it has been tried and experienced as remedies for generations. My grandmother was convinced about the power of many traditional recipes for health and beauty. That's why we keep using them.

I still remember the rice flour we used for face powder. My grandmother made this on a monthly basis. She rolled it into round shape like a marble, sun-dried it, then put it in a mason jar ready to use. She would mix it with rose water and use it daily. I can still envision the feeling of my grandmother's soft skin. I learned more about the power of the mangosteen after I met this customer. I was eager to research it further. It felt as if I had found some hidden treasure. Interesting how human-beings are. We tend to take things for granted when we have them in abundance. In the past, I never had the need to find out more about the mangosteen. It's in season twice a year in Indonesia, plenty to enjoy. I grew up drinking, using and applying traditional recipes as part of a ritual, especially for women. I didn't appreciate it as much until I couldn't find it as easily anymore, until it took thirty-three hours of flying time to enjoy it. It took someone to pop the question to make me realize what I so fortunately had in abundance growing up. I suddenly could hear my grandmother's voice, "Drink this, go back to school tomorrow." She didn't buy my excuse to ditch school.

I didn't know whether I was subconsciously missing my home country, being nostalgic about my childhood, or just pleasantly surprised that someone had asked of a fruit nobody in this part of the world had known before. I suddenly felt the urge to bring it back into my life. I ordered the juice. Charlie and I started consuming it on a daily basis. And then in the next few weeks, I suddenly saw a few other mangosteen products in the market at a couple of places I shopped. "This is weird. Suddenly, the mangosteen products show up out of the blue. How come I never noticed it before?" I asked Charlie. Have you heard people say, "You never notice a yellow car on the road until you drive one?" What you focus on, expands.

Even though we tried all the other products we found, I told Charlie we should stick with the one we learned about from the Minneapolis customer. The product from Utah was the one that reminded me the most about what my grandmother made. The color, the consistency, even the smell, seemed to be similar. Three months afterward, Charlie started experiencing some great health results. We have become a regular consumer ever since. It's our staple, I don't see we will ever stop. I feel I'm keeping my grandmother's legacy alive. After experiencing the continuous benefits of the mangosteen juice, I started sharing it with others.[5] The benefits compounded not only health-wise, but also mind-wise.

Through promoting and sharing this product, I met many wonderful people -- those who were not only taking action to be well, but also to grow and expand mentally. My library has improved dramatically, and I got the opportunity to listen to and meet true teachers at heart, those who sincerely wanted to help me be successful. I realized how important learning was, it's part of growing. When I stop learning, I stop growing. I once felt that school degree was a passport to success. Then I met a number of people through this entrepreneurial journey, who didn't have the luxury of swimming in education, yet had the desire and tenacity to make their dreams a reality. These are the people who inspire me – their *why* and dreams are so real, their purpose is larger than themselves, that the *how* appears to help move them forward. Often times, I get sidetracked by the little things that bug me. I get easily irritated and try to fix it, and in the process I lose sight of my original goal.

As someone who tried to control everything in life, I had lots of rules of engagement. Speaking of the devil, it followed me to Duluth and showed its face many times in our married life. For example, when I cook, I clean up as I cut and chop, so when the food is ready and we're sitting down, I don't leave the kitchen in chaos. I just can't enjoy the food when it is. Charlie, on the other hand, uses the whole kitchen space when cooking; pans and pots, drips and spoons will still be on the counter when we're sitting down and eating. Another example is when we travel, I don't pack or mix clean clothes with dirty clothes and shoes. Dirty clothes will be in laundry bags and shoes will be in bags as well. I'm very territorial about them being in my suitcase. I never put my purse or bag on the floor unless I know for sure it's clean. At one point, Charlie tried to defend himself by saying, "OK now, Sweetie, that's rule #241." I was beginning to think that East and West didn't seem to see eye to eye in a lot of things. These rules, though some make sense and can hang around, can also invade our comfort. They become obstacles to enjoying what's more important in life.

I felt my rules have lessened a lot since moving to Duluth. Life was much more structured and rigid when I was in Indonesia. Of course, Charlie has no way to see the difference. I needed to have rules then so I could get things accomplished. I ran my single life there. I could do things the way I wanted. Now this life is shared with someone else. It hasn't been easy to let go of the rules I lived with for a very long time. I could see how this way of living would slow down or distract me from staying focused on my intention and goals. I sweat the small stuff too much.

Charlie has been a student of Jim Rohn's, America's foremost business philosopher. I had never heard of Rohn until I moved to Duluth. Charlie unintentionally introduced him to me. When we took a road trip, he always listened to Rohn on tape, and I became his captive audience. It was not by choice. Slowly but surely, Rohn's teaching seeped into my consciousness. I became one of his students as well, and our car turned into a university on wheels. There were so many wise nuggets in his teaching that didn't mean much the first few times I heard them. And then one day, I was at the right time and the right place just as I was growing my mangosteen as a business. Rohn hit the nail on the head in many instances. I either was experiencing the challenges he referred to in his speech, or needing the inspiration to keep me on stream.

I had so much access to inspiring books, CDs, and research findings I didn't cross paths with before. Or maybe, I wasn't looking for them then. I wasn't searching to grow. I was busy doing. It's funny how I could hear something at one time, yet it didn't make a dent, and then years later I heard the same thing again, and the light bulb went on. I was definitely at the right time and the right place. But most importantly, I was in the right frame of mind. I was ready. The ground was ready for the seeds to grow. I was reminded of a saying in advertising way back when, "It takes six to seven exposures before someone gets your message." We used this term a lot to help our clients understand the importance of consistency when advertising. I got the memo now. I can't let my mind go dormant and lazy. I need to keep feeding it with great nutrition.

I continued reaching out to inspirational, entrepreneurial and leadership books. I aligned myself with positive energy from friends who were supportive. My dad once told my brother and me, "You might never leave your small home town, but your mind should continue traveling the world." He was a perfect example of that. He called our hometown his home all his life, but he truly traveled the world -- in person and through the many books and magazines to which he subscribed. He remained a student all his life. I now became a student of health and life. My teachers were people: in the books I read, CDs I listened to, and those I met in person, both ordinary and world-renowned. People, whose stories have become a great influence in my life. Network marketing is truly a business of self-discovery and self-development, with great products attached to it.

KEY #3:
DANCING IN THE WISDOM OF YOGA

Our import business started out in a corner of a warehouse in the Western part of Duluth. At the beginning, we focused on wholesale markets, but then an offer we couldn't refuse lured us into opening a retail store in a touristy area of the city. We were growing quite well, most of our big customers were from St. Paul and Minneapolis areas. We even shipped furniture on pallets to decorate winter homes in Florida and California. We traveled quite consistently; at least once a year to Indonesia to get our inventory full, and then twice a year to different markets in the United States to promote it. We developed wonderful relationships with both our suppliers in Indonesia and our retail clientele in North America. It was an experience we cherished much, promoting items and sharing stories behind our unique products. Charlie and I were like cultural ambassadors to Indonesia. Customers and suppliers became our friends.

I worked at the store daily, and then came home to be in contact with our suppliers in Indonesia, where it would be day time there. For two months in the winter and fall we would be on the road to three different markets working the wholesale part of the business, dragging a trailer full of display items. After we returned from the market we would start shipping orders to retailers. That was hard work, physically, but aches and soreness were easily washed away by great feedback and repeat orders from our clients. Work pressure started creeping back up on me, slowly. It was easily brushed away when I was super busy juggling the day and night work load between two countries. I had to do it because I was the only one who could communicate with the Indonesian end of the business.

Now I was becoming more aware of the cycle. I noticed the symptoms of work-related stress quicker. They surfaced and felt familiar. I realized I had to do something. I looked for ways to keep my sanity intact. I needed to calm down the busy chatter in my mind. Toward the end of 2008, while taking a break from decorating the house for the season, I came across the Veria Living channel, which since has become ZLiving on television.

This wellness-focused network offers all natural approach to well-being; from health, beauty, DIY tips, home and natural remedies, food and cooking, as well as fitness. They offered an hour-long *Yoga for Life*[6] session, almost daily, with Kurt Johnsen. For a few days, I woke up early in the morning to catch the show. Soon afterward, I got the hang of it. I wasn't usually a person who made New Year's resolutions, but I made yoga mine. On the second day of January 2009, I started my consistent rendezvous with yoga. I recorded all shows and then did it in rotation. I had a date with yoga from the comfort of our living room, every morning, at six o'clock. Within a month I was becoming more aware of my breathing -- from the core, the valuable benefit of proper breathing that truly refreshed me. Yoga had tremendously helped me not only to stay toned and fit, but most importantly, to stay calm. Within three months, I was becoming used to breathing from my stomach, instead of shallow breathing from the chest. I slept much deeper at night.

I have been a regular to yoga ever since. It's an hour-long meditation as I flow from one pose to another, dancing with life. As he guides me through the class, Johnsen also shares much wisdom that allows me to connect with my body through breathing. "Your breath is a reflection of your peace of mine," he says. I have become more aware when I'm rushing my breathing even though I'm not running. At first, I made an effort to remember breathing from my stomach. And then one day, I caught myself breathing consistently from the core. Breathing correctly had become part of me.

Over time, I also caught myself smiling more often; while driving, walking on the street or just being present in the moment. Smiles rubbed off on me because Johnsen always reminded his class to smile while doing a pose. Do you know how much smiling can affect your day? I heard about smile pep-talk from different sources; magazine, books, thoughts of the day, emails, and friends. I didn't know what to make of it, because I never experienced it. And then I started doing yoga with Johnsen consistently, and slowly, it was changing me. I became a believer in smiling even as soon as I got up in the morning, and greeting myself in the mirror. One thing led to another and the smile never left my face. It followed me to wherever I went that day. It's infectious. Other people I crossed paths with started smiling at me. That's a fabulous way to start an epidemic of smiles.

The way Johnsen reminds us of it is so unpretentious. It's not patronizing. It's part of his convincing yet calming voice as he's guiding his class through poses. The first time I experienced it, it was during a pose when I had to stand on one foot, the other foot was bent on the knee, hands were raised then opened up, eyes on the sky. As I was trying to balance myself from falling, I heard him say, as if he was right in front of me, "Smile," I couldn't help but do so, "Have fun," he continued. After that experience, I often caught myself smiling every time I was falling, in an attempt to strike a challenging pose or was struggling to keep my balance. The more I weaved yoga into my morning routine, the more I realized that a smile automatically appeared after a fall. Then later, the morning practice with Johnsen started trickling into my life outside of my living room.

I used to get easily upset when I failed, when things didn't go according to my expectations, when patience was thin. During my stressful life in advertising, I was known to be a serious person, and behind my back was nicknamed Iron Lady. Now, more often than not, I will smile when things go wrong, or at least try not to frown. If I do get upset, it goes away very quickly. A few years ago, I had a mini reunion with Ditta. We hadn't seen each other, in person, for more than three years,

even though we skyped and chatted on the phone quite regularly. I flew out to New York City when I knew she was going to
be in the Big Apple for a month, and stayed with her for a week.
We were truly catching up on life, even chatting till past
midnight, in bed, before we went to sleep.

The day I was leaving, on my way out of her apartment, she
said, "I'll walk you down," and we continued chatting in the
elevator until we got out of the apartment building. She then
hugged me goodbye and said to me, "You look so peaceful and
content. I've never seen this part of you before." The statement
caught me by surprise, and also moved me. "Let's make a plan
to visit again in Duluth before too long," she promised. She was
the first person from Indonesia who visited me, three months
after I moved to Duluth. I went back to New York City six
months after that short, yet meaningful conversation -- for her
funeral. That was the first time someone from my past noticed
my transformation, I treasured those precious seconds with her.
It's interesting to realize how an opportunity to step away from
a vicious cycle of life had opened doors for me to step toward a
better person. When the mind is at peace and has room to
expand, nutritious ideas can come in and play.

A year ago, I had to clean up and organize my laptop. Over
the years, I had saved photos from life's occasions, articles I
liked and thought I would need some day (but never did),
recipes, forwarded emails from friends, not to mention work-
related files I needed to save. When I bought the laptop brand
new, I had so much space on it. And then five years later the
laptop started giving me problems. It took so long to boot up, it
slowed down for no reason, it froze up in the middle of a
presentation, it truly aggravated me. The computer man told
me that I had crowded up the hard drive, "Say goodbye to
things you don't need, or move them to an external hard drive

for later use," he suggested. I agreed to trash unnecessary old files. He cleared up the chaos and made room for important files to be easily found. Suddenly, the desktop looked nice and tidy, there was room for little icons to move around and breathe. This happened to me twice in the past twelve years. The last time I brought home my laptop from a repair, the computer man sent me home with a piece of paper that listed what I needed to do daily, weekly and monthly. Sure enough, it prolongs the life of the laptop and definitely prolongs my sanity. How true this example is for other parts of my life as well.

The same year I discovered yoga, Charlie and I were faced with a situation that required a serious decision, the one that changed the course of our journey forward. By now, the import business had swallowed much of the bitter taste of the global financial downturn that started a year earlier. We finally reached a decision to pull the plug on the business we had built for seven years. There was a lot of shame that came along with losing a business, even though we could rationalize it – the economy tanked, homes were foreclosed, and buying furniture and home decor wasn't on the top of people's priority list. There was understandably no foot traffic into the stores and no retailers wanted to stock up on inventory. We hung on to it for a year after the economic downturn started, in hopes the situation would turn around. It didn't do so soon enough. We felt as if a sharp knife had poked into our pride and took away the investment, energy, hard work and dreams we built and nurtured, and left behind the regrets and blame -- should've-could've-would've.

I remember reading one of Napoleon Hill's famous books *Think and Grow Rich* a few years earlier. Charlie shared this book with me earlier in our marriage. In search of some wisdom after we closed down the import business, I picked up this book again. And I found it. One of the secrets of success Hill shared was about the importance of having a mastermind group of like-minded people, people we surround ourselves with. When two or more minds working in harmony, he said, they will produce a synergistic energy that creates reality. "... they place themselves in position, through that alliance, to absorb power directly from the greatest universal storehouse of Infinite Intelligence. This is the greatest of all sources of power."[7] This was one of the books I need to revisit every so often. There is always something I overlooked and could relearn.

When Charlie and I were building our business, as small-business owners, we were partners, operators, runners, buyers, sellers. We wore many hats. We didn't have board of directors. We didn't work with a coach or mentor. And, we didn't have a mastermind team. I realized later that this was a typical life of many small business owners. It's so easy to get entangled in everyday operations. We got caught up in *running* the business, instead of *growing* the business. We had to do almost everything ourselves to keep the door open. My to-do list was growing longer every day. When the external storm hit us – in this case, the economic downturn -- we collapsed with it, our internal system wasn't strong enough. We didn't build a storm-proof business.

I had never owned the word peaceful when I lived in Indonesia. I was aware of it. I read about it. I heard people mention it. I heard the sound of it in my mind. But, it was so far away from reality. I couldn't feel it, so I removed it from my vocabulary -- not intentionally. It was out of sight, so eventually it was out of mind. Now this lovely feeling started making some appearances. It appeared when Charlie and I sat in our backyard, in the quiet, listening to nature exchanging morning talks. It came out when I saw the Lift Bridge standing still from a distance, or the gentle waves on Lake Superior dancing elegantly. It showed up when I saw someone hold the door for another person, regardless whether it was a man or a woman. I hardly ever heard a car honk, definitely no middle finger flying around. People often asked me what I thought about Duluth, "It must be quite a shock for you to move here." They then looked at me in disbelief when my answer was simply, "Peaceful." They must have thought I was trying to be nice, "Even after you experienced winter?"

I know this peace was a gradual result of yoga. I was having an hour-long vacation of the mind almost every morning, helping me start the day with the right mindset. In Indonesia, I didn't feel I was stressful, of course, until someone asked me the question, "What's wrong with you?" The question made me even more irritated instead of soothing me down. I'm not sure whether because it was asked with a tone of accusation, or I was just reading too much into it because I was stressed. Another time, I caught myself automatically switching into a complaining mode when a friend I met, while I was out and about, asked me," How's work?" Or, at times I noticed myself sleep binging -- I would sleep twelve to fourteen hours on weekends. Then one day I received a cute card from a colleague of mine, the cover said "If you read STRESSED backward, it spelled DESSERTS". In the inside she wrote, "Let's have some. Don't fuss the little thing." She was the one who introduced me to AsiaWorks.

It's amazing how healthy proper breathing affects my well-being. Long deep breath nurtures my body, clears the clutter in my mind, and freshens my soul. And then one day I realized the weight I carried was lighter. Moving to a new place halfway around the world had allowed me to start a journey within, as well as exploring life's abundant potential. Yoga gave me a tool

– breathing -- to reconnect with myself and hear the question, "What's meaningful in life?" I could feel my life continuing to transform.

KEY #4:

EXPANSION THROUGH MEDITATION

One morning, Charlie and I were traveling to Minneapolis, and Jim Rohn's voice of wisdom was accompanying our trip, "Success is nothing more than a few simple disciplines, practiced every day ...." We looked at each other and smiled. We'd heard this often enough now. The more I listened to Rohn, the more I would catch myself saying *I missed that part before.* Interesting, when the mind is given a chance to rest and clear up, it can see and hear well, then remember better. Listening to his teaching, in the quiet of our moment, allowed us to embrace it even deeper. I recognize the significance of not letting my mind go idle, and the importance of a mentor, or coach, in my life.

One late summer evening, while watching Oprah on television, I was glued on a segment she had about TM, short for Transcendental Meditation.[8] I had never heard of it before, but the show was so intriguing that I mentioned it to Charlie. "We should consider it for this year's personal growth pursuit for us." I went to their website and got myself familiar with what it was. As I was cruising the site, a chat box popped up. "Would you like to chat with a certified TM teacher?" it asked me. The chat led me to a conclusion that we had to go to St. Paul, the nearest center available, to take the course. There were no certified teachers in Duluth. I took notes, shared my phone number with the staff, and mentioned that my husband and I would discuss it further. Both Charlie and I always had a very busy summer with our businesses. It's challenging to get away for a week. But I knew we would get on with it one way or another. Six months later, my phone rang and someone introduced herself as a certified TM teacher from the center. She said there were a few people who were interested in taking the course. She would come up and conduct a class in Duluth.

Twenty minutes of meditation, twice a day, started to show its impact on my everyday life. Gradually, I realized I was able to step back and let go of things. Meditation helped me create a space between me and my response. I wasn't as reactive anymore. With it, I'm growing more aware of my thoughts. I started inching inward to connect with my soul, my deepest me. A spiritual relationship with myself was renewed. I was transforming into a being that was more aware of my presence. Slowly, I started to let go of prerequisites for any good action I needed to do, excuses became more identifiable. Then, great things seemed to have found their way to me -- one good thing after another.

In the past, especially when I was still involved in the advertising world, I was prone to dive in and fix something, simply because I wasn't patient enough to let things evolve. I couldn't wait to comment on something I suspected wouldn't be right, or correct. It's like watching a movie, I gave away the ending to those who were still watching so we could move on. I seemed to be able to predict what someone was going to say, and it usually wouldn't be what I thought. Instead of listening attentively, I was busy with my own thoughts, designing a clever comeback to prove the other person's thought wasn't correct. I didn't allow the process to run its course. I took shortcuts, put words into people's mouths, and showed them the final outcome. I must have strangled lots of budding thoughts and ideas from flourishing. Looking back at it, I can even hear my tone of voice was always in a hurry. Everything was urgent, wasting time was a sin.

Slowly, Transcendental Meditation started clearing up my overloaded mind, the control, the possessiveness. At first, it was challenging to keep my mind quiet during a meditation. There seemed to be lots of ideas dancing around. "Don't fight the thought, let it be there. Let it come and go," the teacher's voice reminded me. It guided me to practice surrendering, by not fighting it, I slowly let go of the grip and calmness took over, naturally, unintentionally. That was the first takeaway I experienced with TM; allowing the body and mind to relax, to not fight what came to mind. It's amazingly joyful coming out the other side of a twenty-minute meditation, a feeling hard to describe. One needs to experience it to know what it is. Each person may have a different experience, even the same person, at different times, may experience different feelings out of it. The biggest win I felt for myself was the ability to let go. It was liberating to be able to inhale the joy of releasing that controlling bondage.

Letting go was the biggest challenge I had to conquer in the past. I hung on to many things, including those of sentimental value. The six-year-old me was caught off guard when my mom was *taken* away. There was no warning. Then the seven-year-old me was *shoved* to a different city and separated from my dad. My little mind was tossed around and confused. Slowly, I started building a control over what I could hang on to. I still have pieces of mom's clothing which fit me and I can still wear -- her traditional *kebaya*[9] and batik *kain panjang*.[10] This seemingly harmless habit later expanded to other things. It hurts me to throw things away. I slowly began to save things. One of them was gift wrappings. Since my childhood, when we received a gift, we would unwrap it very carefully so we could reuse the wrapper. Some people might say, "That's good, that's recycling." Then when I had passed my teenage years, it expanded into food. "There are many children in Africa who can't and don't have anything to eat. Be appreciative of what you have, finish what you put on your plate," was a signature tune I heard often when I was growing up. Some might still think this was a benign habit. But then, it grew wider and invaded shopping bags, mason jars, rubber bands, and the list slowly became longer. I was a hoarder. A deceiving one. No one would notice it because everything was neatly kept.

When I moved to Duluth, I brought a lot of things from Indonesia to surround myself with home; the smell of batik cloth, incense, and candles soothed my mind. The sound of bamboo chimes brought peace to my ears. The batik bed cover kept my memory from slipping away. Sometimes, in trying not to run out of things that reminded me of my home country, I was stingy in using them. "Let's enjoy them, so they keep bringing home to you," Charlie bargained with me. I was afraid not to be able to have them again if we used too much of them too fast. I felt I needed to hang on to them longer. I was afraid when they were gone, I would lose my connection to home as well. The idea of losing something valuable and important was still a difficult experience for me to comprehend. "Just let me hold on to them a little longer," I counter-bargained in my mind, "Using them would eventually finish them," I continued rationalizing. It gave me enough solace knowing I had them within reach. They were available, even though they were still in boxes, in the basement storage room. Meditation slowly loosened up my grip, very gently so that it didn't startle me. I wasn't even aware of it until I reached the other side of letting go.

When Charlie and I downsized our life, biding adieu to a three-floor, four-bedroom house and moving into a one-level, two-bedroom condominium unit, we had to let go of so much stuff through an estate sale. In the process of doing so, I found many unopened boxes in our basement storage room, which came with me from Indonesia ten years earlier. I knew we couldn't fit all of them in our much smaller new home, so I gave Charlie the authority to decide. "Don't tell me what you find in those boxes, just let go of things you think I won't miss." I opted not to even look at them, I calmed myself down by saying, "If I don't remember it, it must have not been important." Charlie screened things a head of time so I didn't need to waste our time going through boxes. With things he wasn't sure about, he would ask me, "What do you remember about this?" He would make a decision based on hearing the story around that particular item. "Ooooh ... we should keep that." Otherwise, I would immediately know I could now let go of it, just by listening to my own voice telling the story. It's an amazing revelation.

Downsizing was the best time to organize life. There's so much I had accumulated in life, material things, shoes, purses, bags, and clothes. At one particular time, I could only wear one or two of them. I couldn't believe I had so many of them. When I was working in advertising, I allocated a budget to expand my wardrobe every few months. Divorcing this army of attire was initially hard, they were wearable, and there's memory attached to each of them. I then learned to dialogue with myself, "How often am I going to wear it?" Most of the attire I brought from Indonesia was suited for the tropics, which could now only be worn comfortably in the summer. The walk-in closet was now smaller in the new home. I had to part ways with things, and it was time to do so. High heels, I hardly wore them now, except for going to parties. A dialogue with myself continued, "How many parties do I go to every year? I could count on one hand." I remember my sister-in-law used to joke about my shoes. She nicknamed me Indonesia's Imelda Marcos. I took great care of my shoes, many of them were ten years old or more. They were in plastic shoe boxes and stacked neatly. They were all marked with short description – style, color. You know how old styles suddenly are trending again, don't you? I tried them on one by one, walked around the house to test how comfortable they still were. The ones that were tighter on my feet could now find their new home. They had accumulated enough mileage with me. They could partner with other feet and start a new journey.

High-heels were not efficient anymore for me. I needed to move around more quickly -- in and out of the car, walking, and running errands. I now spent a lot more time outdoors compared to the time when I was still living in Indonesia. I remember friends commenting how tan I was when I went back to visit Indonesia. "You're now living in a four-season environment, how can that be?" Indonesia is a humid country. The temperature ranges between 70F to 100F all year round. Spending time outdoors was just uncomfortable. I worked in an air-conditioned office, and I was in and out of an air-conditioned car. It's totally the opposite life here in the Northland. Summer is short. Consequently, when it comes, we want to enjoy the outdoors as much as we can. Living lighter is healthier. Decluttering makes life simpler and more comfortable.

The first Christmas since we moved into the condominium in downtown Duluth, Charlie and I made a commitment to include personal improvement as our annual goal. Instead of allocating a budget for attire, or other trivial things, I'm now allocating a budget for books and inspiring CDs. Our Christmas list had a facelift and was directed toward nurturing the mind, body and spirit. The first door that was opened to me -- moving to Duluth – had springboarded to other vigorous ways of living. I started to feel I enjoyed my life even more. I wasn't busy just doing things, I took time to breathe life. Suddenly, my brother's comment from a long time ago made more sense now. I didn't need to be busy doing things to be productive. Meditation is basically not doing anything -- sitting still with eyes closed, letting go of mind chatter without trying. Yet, it's such a productive activity. It allows the mind, *the brain*, to rest and be calm. As a result, it becomes productively healthy.

KEY #5:
STUDENTSHIP, FROM HERE TO ETERNITY

Jim Rohn continues beaming wisdom into my mind, "We are the average of the five people we spend the most time with." We're influenced by the people we surround ourselves with -- they affect our feelings and thoughts, our decisions, our growth and our success. By the same token, we're also affected by the thoughts we think the most -- be it negative or positive. We're also affected by the result of our action, forward or backward. I have encountered life through books I read and mind-growing people I meet, I have experienced peace with yoga, I have felt joy with meditation, and I have seen my true being showing up in the process. Those are the five elements of life I'll continue surrounding myself with – books, people, yoga, meditation, and the growing me.

One April day, while Charlie and I were having a session with our health coach, she asked me, "Something new you'd like to explore this year?" Interesting question, I thought. Yes, I had been thinking about it. Charlie and I had agreed to grow one step better each year. "I've always wanted to learn more about nutrition," I thought out loud. "Tell me more, what do you mean by that?" she looked at me. "I had always been

fascinated to learn about it," I responded, "I watched my grandmother using herbs and plants without knowing why they did
what they did. She just knew they would be good." I stopped
and took a deep breath. "I'm curious." A pause followed silently.
"But I don't see myself going to a two-year, or four-year, school.
It's not that kind of schooling I'm looking for." Another pause, I
was truly thinking out loud. "I want to take a journey within,
finding out what nourishes me, and why." That's it, I heard
myself.

She handed me a leaflet and said, "Check this out." I
glanced through it quickly, and smiled. It was a leaflet about
the Institute for Integrative Nutrition®, or IIN®. The word
integrative caught my eyes. On the way out of the room, I overheard Charlie share his final thought of the session with the
health coach, "I bet you, she'll check it out tonight." And I did.
And I registered for a free information webinar, which happened to be available right on the following day. "Wow," I
thought, the Universe certainly didn't waste time on this one.
The webinar hit the right button. It seemed to have answered
all the questions that were floating in my mind these past few
years, or few months. Whatever it was, this might be what I
have been looking for. "The law of attraction works when you're
in action." Yes, yes, I heard you. I had been searching. There are
no coincidences in life. It was meant to be, because I searched
for it, and the Universe honored it.

Let me first share my interesting experience with the
Universe. Six months prior to my meeting with our health
coach, a friend from my mastermind alliance club suggested a
book entitled *E-Squared: Nine Do-It-Yourself Energy Experiments That Prove Your Thoughts Create Your Reality*, by Pam
Grout. The first experiment in this book is about a request for
an unexpected gift from the Universe. I had to define my

request, but I didn't get to specify what it was and how it happened. So, I asked to be surprised by something I hadn't thought about. The book suggested that I jot down the time when I launched the intention -- it was Sunday, November 24th 2013, nine o'clock in the evening, Duluth time. I would also be taking notes and documenting the findings. The time required for this experiment was forty-eight hours. I was honestly excited to welcome whatever came my way.

The next morning, I had an early meeting and then ran some errands to get prepared for Thanksgiving. I got home around eleven o'clock, I totally forgot about the experiment, turned on my laptop, and checked some emails. One of them was a notification from Facebook that someone in Indonesia had sent a note to me. The note said; "Are you Inge who used to work in FCB?" – this was the advertising agency I worked for before I moved to Duluth. I looked at the name. I didn't recall anyone by that name, so I responded to her, "Yes, I am. I'm sorry I don't recognize your name. Did you also work in FCB?" A day after that first encounter, I received a lengthy note in my inbox from her, and here's what she said, translated into English:

"No, I never worked in FCB. I don't know whether you remember us, both my sister and I remember you quite clearly, although your face seems blurry now. I have your business card with me, which I have kept for a very long time. In 2006, I was working for a telecommunication company and found out that our company was using FCB as its advertising agency. I then asked my friend who was in close contact with the agency people to find out whether you were still working there. My friend reported back saying that you had moved to the United States a few years ago. I thought, 'There goes my chance to meet you again.' But

then, yesterday I was cleaning my room and sorting out stuff we wanted to get rid of – we're in the process of moving – and your business card reappeared. In this day and age we go to Google or Facebook to help us find someone we lost contact with. I searched for your name, and there you were. I was hoping it was you."

There was a reason she wanted to reconnect with me. On one Sunday afternoon, sometime in July 1999, she was at the mall with her sister. "While we were deciding on where to have lunch, suddenly someone tapped my shoulder. This person introduced herself and invited us to lunch," she told me on her note. That person, apparently, was me. She said she was a little suspicious, but went along with me anyway. When we finally parted ways, she said I gave her my business card and asked her not to hesitate to contact me if there was anything I could do to assist her with her intention to pursue a career in advertising. What would be the odds of my tapping someone's shoulder who was thinking about a career in advertising?

That Sunday afternoon was the last day of my Basic program with AsiaWorks. There were roughly 400 people who took this course and *that* afternoon we were asked to go to public places and were given an hour to connect with someone. There were about a hundred people who succeeded and I was one of them. The purpose of the task was to go out of our way, reach out to a stranger, and offer assistance. In an ordinary situation, I would have put limitations on myself for fear people would think I was crazy, weird, or up to no good. As a result, I might have pushed away great opportunities that might have come my way. I have had many of those instances in the past. I went back to Facebook to see at what time she sent the first note to me. It was Sunday night at 11:15, Duluth time, two hours and fifteen minutes after I launched the intention. Three months after that first reconnection through Facebook, I went back to Indonesia for a visit and we reconnected in person. Since that experience, I became more aware of sending my intention to the Universe. Pam Grout mentioned in her book that, "... there is a loving, abundant, totally hip force in the Universe. Some people call it God."[11] I was to demand a clear, unmistakable sign, something that couldn't be written off as a coincidence. And I was pleasantly surprised.

In the past, I often doubted myself. One example, there was an opportunity to join a conference to learn and be around a community of entrepreneurs who educate, empower and support business leaders. There was a cost, of course, to join this conference. It was a hefty price, but there were also ways to overcome this challenge. I gave up before I even tried. The price overpowered me in such a way that I sacrificed the opportunity to be around not just big-name people, but people who had walked the path to success and truly intended to pull beginners up to walk with them. I was caught up in a panic dialogue with myself, "That's darn expensive. What if it takes years to pay back the cost? What if I don't find a mentor who can help me? What if I drowned in a sea of attendees and no one notices me?" There were lots of what-ifs cluttering my mind. The Universe was confused, "Did you really want to go and take advantage of the conference? Which one do you want?" Each of my doubts was a message to the Universe. I wasn't single-minded with what I really wanted. The Universe was at a loss as to which one to grant. I got caught up with coming to terms with the *how* instead of the *why* I wanted to be there. The Universe will provide the *how*, it's been proven to me on many occasions, the *how* appears. I just need to be ready, truly want to step forward, and the road will show up.

IIN® came to me.

No, let me rephrase the sentence, "I was searching, I was open, I launched my intention. I was curious about nutrition, but it wasn't the typical school that I was looking to go to." I was ready. The student was ready, so the teacher showed up. IIN® has been there all along. They have been empowering people for twenty-three years to claim and own their health. I didn't see it before, I never heard of it, until I launched my intention. That was the biggest win I learned from meditation. I learned to let go, to have an intention but letting go of how it comes to me. For someone who grew up being a control freak, this is huge progress to realize -- how far I had grown.

Suffice it to say, I started my journey with IIN® two weeks after I received a leaflet from my health coach. And a whole course of an amazing journey branched out for me to take in. I was evolving, and I could feel it. I was aware of my transformation, it was flashing bigger and more exciting as I went through each module steadily -- every week, every lecture, every book I read, every peer coaching and coaching circle I was a part of. Every week, it was like opening a gift and being surprised by what I found. It wasn't just about what I initially wanted to learn – which was nutrition -- but also what I didn't know I could explore abundantly to heal my body, and mind – which was nutrition that comes from sources other than food.[12]

I was struck by life's greatest gift of health – the gift of getting in tune with this smart body of mine. My education had programmed me since a very young age to look for answers, for knowledge. The sources mostly were from outside of me – teachers, books, parents, grownups, science, et cetera. My grandmother was an advocate of healthy living naturally. But when she passed on and my life was swimming with modern technology, I lost touch with the ability to really listen to my own body. As part of society, I was relying too much on others to fix me, instead of taking responsibility to make changes. I was becoming a person who was waiting and expecting things to happen to me.

I made a commitment to myself. I set an intention to take a journey within, to understand myself and my body. I started experiencing a difference in the first quarter of schooling. I was delighted to discover what my body was telling me. I was overwhelmed with excitement. As I was moving forward to the second quarter, I suddenly realized my surrounding was changing with me. I was dancing in harmony with life – some dances were sharp and passionate like an Argentinean tango, some were smooth and flawless like a Venetian waltz – and I didn't want to leave the dance floor. From diving inward to discover how my body would respond, the energy now brought me outward to reach out and invite others to dance with me. Without realizing it, I was joining the many IIN® health coaches on the dance floor – learning from their experiences about their own discoveries. We were learning to guide each partner to immerse in the music of love, health, happiness, joy and peace. This was the last key that opened a new door and signified my transformation.

I started a new partnership with my body; how I treat it, the food I bring into it, the conversations I have with it, what it loves or doesn't love having, what-when-why it craves certain foods or activities, and when it needs to rest. Now, I shouldn't be surprised anymore with what I receive in return. This joyful, peaceful, and healthy body allows my mind and spirit – me -- to explore life's abundant possibilities. I used to have doubts about my comprehension and ability in using English, my second language. Somehow, doubts often got in the way. I was busy thinking about how people would respond to me, especially over the phone, when they heard my accent. I knew, because of that, I didn't project myself confidently as often as I wanted to. My doubt had clouded my mind and slowed down my actions. I had excuses for not doing something important for my business or my personal growth. IIN® intensive coaching system, in a group and with a peer coach, allows me to practice, listen, embrace and give feedback, and then improve.

I saw a new horizon when I moved to a new home, and a new life, in Duluth. Like a fish that was swimming in a big pond, with many fish big and small when I was in Indonesia, I was then transferred to a fresher pool, a smaller fish bowl, but it has a fresher environment. And I grew healthier. This healthier environment allows me to swallow healthier food for the body, mind, and spirit. And every day afterward, I'm more in tune with myself, my existence, my passion and my life's journey forward. It's a transformation that's happening naturally. It's like a snowball rolling forward, getting bigger and building momentum. I didn't force it to happen, I flew along with it. That's how I make sense of Jiddu Krishnamurti's quote I shared at the beginning of this chapter -- *"If you begin to understand what you are without trying to change it, then what you are undergoes a transformation."* — I began to understand what I was when I moved to America, I began to see that something was not quite right. As I inched forward, the path became clearer. And then one day I realized, the mind was ready, then the body followed effortlessly, and the spirit propelled me upward. I was transformed.

Jim Rohn's voice of wisdom returned to me. I heard this story the first time through a lady mentor of mine in my mangosteen business. One day, she went to Rohn's seminar and was able to sit next to him during dinner. She told Rohn how excited she was to be able to meet the person who had changed her life for the better. She was overcome with gratitude. Rohn patiently listened to her and when she was done he said to her -- I'm paraphrasing – "Thank you for thinking I was the reason you had changed. I might be the one that pushed the right button, but I wasn't alone. You had taken many steps in the past that finally brought you to me. Imagine there was a box that required a five-key combination to open it. I happened to be that last key, so the floodgate was released and you flourished abundantly. But I wouldn't be able to do so unless you had gone through and found the first four keys. It took five to open the box. You searched and found the four keys yourself, you went through the journey, and I am honored to have helped you find the last one." She was transformed.

Now I was listening to that story one more time as I was listening to Jim Rohn's CD in the car. I had found my last key in IIN®. I could now relate to that story, personally.

ᏕᎭᏟᎡ

"If you want to fly on the sky
you need
to leave the earth.
If you want to move forward,
you need
to let go the past
that drags you down."

Amit Ray
World Peace:
The Voice of a Mountain Bird

ᏕᎤᏯ

MEMORY LANE REVISITED: LESSONS LEARNED

The trip to Pittsburg, Kansas, had opened the door for me to understand the paths I've walked on, and how they affect my journey forward. This was the first trip I took with Charlie, where I could see how I responded to him, to things, as opposed to reacting to them like I used to do. This was the first time I could feel my new self show up in a way that I felt "I truly am here, I am present." It was a wonderful feeling to have arrived at, and I was beginning to enjoy having and spending time with me, my true self. In February 2014, I went back to Indonesia, alone, for a month. This was a long overdue visit since 2008. I hadn't seen my brother and his family, in person, for more than five years. We did use the magic of technology and social media to stay connected, but this was the first time we would see and be around each other again after a long time. One of his two children had grown almost as tall as the parents, the other was taller. My nephew's voice had changed, he'd grown into a reserved young man, unlike his cheerful and talkative young self.

93

A couple of days after my arrival, we had a gathering with close friends and my sister-in-law mentioned something that made me aware I was no longer the person I used to be. She shared with the group what and how she felt when I greeted her. "She looked and sounded different; her eyes and tone of voice radiated vibes I hadn't seen in her before," she said. I didn't know what to make of it at that point. It made me think I wasn't somebody she felt at ease to be around. Even my vibes, my energy, must have been forceful back then. Suddenly, Ditta's remark when I visited her in New York City reemerged. She also saw a different me, she felt I was at peace. And now, during this trip with Charlie, I saw a new me in a way people who were close to me were experiencing lately. That was an epiphany.

I had been itching to move onward and upward, a few times in life. I didn't quite know at the beginning why I was ready. I wasn't comfortable where I was personally and the state of mind I was in. I felt I was dragged, swirled, and bounced around on the baggage carousel of life. One turn after another, it seemed so fast that I couldn't get off it. Then after a while, I was hypnotized by the rhythm of life. I got lost in the constant process of moving, even though I was basically stationary. The carousel was going in a circle and would finally pass the same spot again, many more times after that. And life went on, and on, and on ... in a circle. I was active doing things, but it wasn't productive. And when I was sucked deeper into the swirl of life, I couldn't hear the calling -- the knock on the door of my heart trying to remind me to slow down, to listen, and to be ready for another sign. I was so busy going in motion, chasing something I thought was important until I was out of breath, and then realized it wasn't what I was looking for after all. I couldn't describe what happiness was back then. I knew that was what I wanted, but I couldn't describe it. The only thing I could hear afterward, was the same chatter of would've-could've-should've.

MAKING PEACE WITH MY PAST

Writing this book has not only been therapeutic, but has also brought back many memories I had forgotten for so long, especially my childhood. Memories that were wrapped around a painful event that was hard to make sense of. I had subconsciously buried these moments deeper in the basement of my being, until I was so detached from them. It was so deep, I didn't have any feeling about them anymore. I remember, throughout my life, a number of people asked me, "How did you feel about that day?" The exact question might be different from one person to another, but the basic message they wanted to know was the same – the feeling of losing a mother. I can now picture myself with a blank stare trying to access the feeling, and then would follow up on the question with, "I can't remember. It was a long time ago." I remembered the details at the church, but I didn't have any recollection about what transpired after that. It was as difficult to find a record of how I felt then.

I know I was, and had always been, alright because I had grownups around me who took care of me. I never remember talking about that confusing day. My dad was thirty-six years old, with three, young children under the age of eight to care for. He did the best he could with the help of relatives. My baby brother was taken care of by my grandmother's youngest sister after he was released from the hospital. *Uma Katjil*, we called her, which means the youngest grandma. She was single, and lived with Mam just a few doors away from where my dad, brother and I lived. My brother and I saw him often, we played with him after school. He was a happy baby, loved by many around him. I can now picture those limited moments of his life; his excited giggle, his highchair by the dining table, his little feet erratically ran in the air when he saw a bowl approaching the table with some goody in it. My happy baby brother was reunited with mom eleven months after he came to earth; bronchitis. That was another blow for the family.

Dad's and mom's families were neighbors. Dad had always been considered a brother by mom's seven siblings, and as one of their own by my grandparents, long before he married mom. They went to the same elementary school. They hung out and played together because they were all so close in age. He became best friends with mom's two youngest brothers. I remember a story dad used to tell. One day, my grandmother gave all her eight children a time out. She lined them up by the wall and whipped their behinds with a rattan stick, one by one. Then she realized, after hearing my grandfather's chuckle from a distance, looking at her trying to discipline the children, that one of them wasn't theirs. Dad overheard her response, "What do I know? Their butts all look the same to me." Even long after my maternal grandparents had passed and dad had remarried, he remained a brother to mom's siblings, and his opinion had always been regarded as important in their family's decisions. This is a lovely memory of mine.

I now understand why my brother and I were sent to live with Mam a little over a year after mom's passing. Surabaya was not only a better city for us to expand our horizon, but also a safer surrounding for us to grow and mature. Mam had a daughter much older than us, and became our older sister. There were also two aunts of Mam's who lived with her to help watch over us. Mam's cousin lived next door, with four sons who were around our age and older. My maternal grandparents were in their seventies by then. The oldest aunt was moving to Germany with her husband, so no grownups were left behind in our small hometown except for some distant relatives. And dad had a busy business to run. These were things a young being couldn't understand. The only thing I knew was, in less than two years, I had lost a mother, a baby brother, and was separated from my dad. Was that little girl's feeling ever acknowledged? We never talked about it, we never addressed it. It's nobody's fault. The grownups did what they knew they could. Understandably, it would be difficult to talk about such a loss with a young person, while the grownups were also grieving.

I recall the talks Mam shared with some relatives, in the presence of my brother and me, surrounding mom's death. A week or two before my baby brother was scheduled to be born, mom had agreed to deliver him in Surabaya instead. There were not enough experienced medical practitioners in our hometown's hospital then. The obstetrician/gynecologist who helped deliver my brother and myself, whose family had been a family friend of ours, was suddenly transferred to a different city just a month prior to our brother's birth. Arrangement had been made. Bags were packed and Mam would accompany her sister to Surabaya. Then just a few days prior to departure, mom cancelled the trip with the reason that she couldn't leave my brother and me at home, even though, she knew there were many family members around: our grandparents, the oldest aunt, an uncle and his wife (my Godparents) who lived a few doors away. She wasn't at peace leaving us, and she decided to deliver our baby brother in town. The family accepted the fact as fate, it was her time, but I can now understand the regret and guilt surrounding the incidence of that first day in April.

There wasn't any grief counseling available in our small

hometown, in the sixties. I don't think the family ever heard of such a therapy either. I, not knowingly, blocked it out of my mind for a very long time until the wound was dry. I had divorced the feelings, emotionally. I only remember learning bits and pieces about it, when I was a teenager, many years after that April Fool's Day. By then, I was numb, no emotional recollection of it. One day, I would like to talk about it with my brother; how much he remembers about the feelings he had of that day, and the days afterward, how he coped with it. He was two years older than I, but still, he was just a boy, short of his eighth birthday. Revisiting this part of my earlier life; remembering what had transpired, imagining what the grownups in my family had to go through then, has helped me understand the person I was, in dealing with the loss, as well as the person I had become, as I moved forward in life. I understand why I became possessive of what I could guard and keep close to me. I felt entitled to things and feelings, within my control. That possessiveness was nurtured and groomed as I was becoming more disciplined and independent.

A few weeks ago, I was deep in my meditation, and I suddenly saw that six-year-old little girl who lost her mother. I was overcome with fresh and raw feelings. When I realized it, I was in tears. It wasn't just sadness, it was tears of relief. I let myself experience the feelings. I reached out to that little girl and embraced her. I acknowledged her feelings. "You are not alone, you are not lost. I have found you." I could amazingly feel the heavy burden slowly being lifted. Now that little girl was at peace. I made peace with my past. I could see the child who sat in the dark corner of a room, with her head buried in the hollow of her knees, for fifty years, is now with me. I hugged her, I felt her heartbeat singing a livelier tune. She wasn't going to be wandering around with no purpose anymore. That journey has ended and a new avenue has opened wide. I hear one word often mentioned at funerals, after I was settling in Duluth. A word I would have never associated with death. The word was *celebrate*, or *celebration*. A long-time friend of Charlie's just lost his dear wife to cancer at that time. In a big and full church, while seeing people around me silently crying and I quietly guarded my own feeling, I heard not only the priest, but also people who shared words about the deceased, remind us to *celebrate* the life she had lived. I remember thinking, "How could you associate death with this word? For God's sake, we just lost someone dear to us." I remember feeling really weird about it, so much so that I wasn't ready to even ask Charlie about it. "Something I need to learn about the culture here," was how I neutralized my thought. Indonesians, in general, mourn quietly. We maintain silence as much as possible, no bright colors displayed. It's definitely far from a celebration. Being at a funeral mass always reminds me of the time I turned my head following my mom's coffin as they carried it out of church. It was a painful moment. I couldn't even try to remember the fun stuff we had done together, let alone celebrating life. But then gradually, as I went to more funerals, I started to embrace the meaning of this word.

As I'm revisiting that April Fool's Day, I can see the word celebration has now a different meaning. My childhood has more stories; it wasn't just about that first of April when I was picked up early from school. I can look at old albums with a joyful smile. There were so many more cheerful moments that have happened in the past five decades, that were over-powered by one painful day. In an unconscious attempt to wipe the pain, I accidently erased the fun, the highlight and successes that were a part of my life. I can now make peace with death, and with losing someone dear to me. I don't want the memory of my mom to be erased; the limited moments I had spent with her, the things we did together. It had been a long time since then, it was time to reconnect with it. And as I go through each page writing this book, I remember the things that were lost. I opened my childhood album a few days ago, and I can remember the way she looked.

Each picture has now turned into a three-dimensional story in my mind. The memories are slowly coming back. I remember the many clothes she made for my brother and me. She loved sewing, and she sewed many of her own clothes as well. Some of them that come alive are the polka-dot black-and-white dress she sewed for me, a sailor-style with a tie in front, which was popular then. And she used the same fabric for my brother's shirt. My mom was a cat-walk model in our simple hometown where Dutch-educated people lived at that time. She was soft-spoken, kind and gentle. I'm digging through my memory storage box and can never remember her raising her voice. The many traditional fabrics she left behind, the ones she wore for different occasions and when she was modeling, they're now with me, as she is. These are memories that never die even though she is gone. These are the moments worth celebrating; her life with us, her smile, her presence as my mom.

Between November 2011 and September 2012, I lost three dear people in my life; two very close friends, both had passed within four months of each other, in New York City. For a while afterward, going to the Big Apple would remind me too much of losing them, too many places and events I used to enjoy talking about with these two dear hearts. Now our inside jokes have no meaning. I guess this will be the memory I will celebrate when I think of them. The last of those three dear people was Mam, in August 2012.

When I went to Germany for Mam's funeral, I was visiting

with the priest the evening before the funeral. He was gathering stories about Mam, from her only grandson, for the funeral sermon. He then turned to me and asked what I remembered most about her. I recall mentioning the word 'celebrate' and seeing his look when he heard it. I immediately followed it up with an explanation, "I have so many stories to capture how much I have learned from her. She was my mother. Her determination, tenacity, and love for others inspire me. Everyone who knew her had become her friend. That's the life we need to celebrate. I'd like to invite those who knew her to remember the experiences they shared with her, and continue celebrating that part of her life to enjoy the value of life and friendship." He smiled at me. The next day, in the middle of his sermon at the funeral mass, which was delivered in German, he looked at me and paraphrased what I said, in English. At that moment, a new definition of death had been shared, and carried forward to another culture, just as I was enlightened with it since I became a part of a life in America. One life may have ended, but the memories will live on. That's worth celebrating.

When my brother and I were involved with a church program for single, young adults in Indonesia, we learned and made the connection that 'who we are now is a product of who we were before'. As facilitators, we kept seeing the effect of this relationship between then and now. I never thought that one day I, myself, would return to my childhood, revisiting the moment of losing my mother, to break free from its invisible pain. My little six-year old self had kept her feelings to herself for way too long. Darkness is a torturing solitude; it's a lonely place to be. I couldn't articulate my feelings then because I didn't know how. The sorrow was magnified a couple more times by the passing of my baby brother, and the separation from my dad. With every event, I buried the pain deeper within me until there was a space between the two. I didn't seem to see it anymore, even though it was still there.

One of the teachers in IIN®, Paul Epstein, ND, made a mention in his lecture about the importance of body-mind connection. He quoted an excerpt from the *Impact of Early Childhood Trauma on Health and Disease: the Hidden Epidemic,* "Traumatic events of the earliest years of infancy and childhood are not lost but, like a child's footprints in wet cement, are often preserved lifelong. Time does not heal the wounds that occur in those earliest years; time conceals them. They are not lost; they are embodied."[13] And the wounds later show up in different places, at different times. The strong grip to hold on to what could be controlled, later spilled over into many aspects of my life; in relationships, at work, with food and health, money and faith.

I arrived in adulthood doing things, keeping busy, so I didn't need to face the silence that was linked to the dark pain of loss. That was what my brother saw, through his observation, when he said, I associated productivity with doing things. I lived a life chasing something; something I thought I would find some-where, some day. I was relentless, I was persistent. It didn't dawn on me that by doing so I took *now* for granted. I didn't value the present. A couple of years ago, I came across Seth Godin's blog that explained the difference between persistence and tenacity. I had a moment of clarity. Here's what he said, "Persistence is doing something again and again until it works. It sounds like 'pestering' for a reason. Tenacity is using new data to make new decisions to find new pathways to find new ways to achieve a goal when the old ways didn't work."[14] Change is needed, most importantly, the willingness to change. Often times, that willingness couldn't appear because life didn't allow it to emerge. The mind was too congested with counter-healthy chatter.

The steps to arrive to here and now had started a few years ago when I encountered yoga. I'm thankful I had the thirst to search. Later, I found out that this first step to finding calmness had helped me springboard to other healthful decisions in life. Jim Rohn's pearls of wisdom whispered an affirmation, "Success is a few simple disciplines practiced every day." It surely is interesting to realize how one simple healthy action can snowball into greater well-being. The consistent practice of yoga has expanded my horizons and allowed me to be more open-minded to good suggestions. I let go of the heavy baggage I didn't realize I had been carrying all my life. I made peace with my past. I forgave what happened, it was unfortunate, but my life is worth living. I said goodbye to the pain and left it behind, but I carry the memory forward. I'm making definite strides onward. It's lighter. It's happier.

LETTING GO OF CONTROL

If you asked people who were close to me about the person I was when I was in college, even through my working career, the word adventurous would never be associated with me. Uptight was probably more easily identified with me. Even my dad and brother used to joke, "C'mon now, laugh with us." When we were on vacation as a family, I often wondered looking at them giggling and laughing over silly things I didn't find funny at all. "What's going on with these two?" I often said to myself. At one point, my brother even said, "I don't think she gets it, she doesn't see the humor in it." No, he wasn't being sarcastic, he just accepted the fact I was seriously removed from lively fun. Later, I would hear similar response from Charlie, trying to tease me, when he saw the look in me indicating that his joke didn't suit my feelings, "Laugh, Sweetie, that was funny." He doesn't

Inge Maskun

do it as often anymore now, because I do laugh with him, and at him, often until I can't even hear my own laugh because my stomach hurts from the laughter.

I can now laugh out loud seeing funny things on television, silly jokes on late-night television, forwarded videos from friends, and just about and around everyday happenings I found unamusing before. It's truly relieving to be able to do that. I can cry and laugh as hard now, because I can feel both. It was the feeling that was missing before, the presence of it. And when I became distant from that feeling, the numbness started invading other parts of my life and eventually occupied a major part of my being. I became unadventurous and unspontaneous. I was uptight.

Yes, I was. How could I not be? I planned things so thoroughly, then stubbornly stuck to it. I went through life checking off my list, one task after another. My life was run like a boot camp, it was structured. I was accomplishing at first, but halfway through life I was drugged by routine. I couldn't shake off the hangover. I can't remember when I wasn't in control. That's how deep and gripping this character was. It's challenging to let go of something that has been embedded in me for so long. It's not my nature to lose a grip because letting go seems like surrendering to the unknown. Even now, even after I've seen enough evidence and have heard feedback from those who have known me long enough to see the change in me. It's still challenging to let go of the grip. I sometimes still hear the voice in my head trying to make sure, "Am I ok with it? Am I letting go of it?" I'm having a constant dialogue with myself to check my state of being. I don't want to let go just because I have to, but because it's a result of an authentic me feeling truly alright with it.

As calmness shows up more frequently, I no longer have

the urge to step in and take matters into my own hands. In the past, it was difficult for me to accept the fact that someone else I was competing against *won*. To me, losing meant not in control. Being indecisive and losing control would equal weakness. I felt lost and naked if I let go of control. Even losing on a leisure game of cards, or cribbage, could tick me off. I hate losing. I wasn't even a good listener. My brain was always thinking about the next question or statement. To be right was important to me, so my finger almost always had to be on the pulse of happenings. I was always in motion, chasing the right answers. But of course, I didn't realize it because I was too stubborn to let go. Reflecting on what was repeatedly happening to me then is like having an out-of-body experience. In trying to control things, even my own feelings, I closed the door to the unexpectedly surprising possibilities. It's like having a business with the sign "closed" hanging up all, or most of, the times. How can customers walk in? I became an experienced bystander who was watching from a distance, but was afraid to open the door or dip my toes in the water of the unknown. While trying hard not to lose control, I was actually losing many chances to experience life's surprises.

This is where yoga, as well as meditation, has helped me tremendously in letting go of control. Just this morning, I was reminded by it. Breathing is essential in yoga, fluid breathing that is. In every yoga session I go through with Kurt Johnsen, I hear him say, "Breathe." Between poses, he encourages me to explore further, yet he also reminds me, "If you lose your breath, back off." By now I know enough that the pose is not the practice; the breath, the state of mind is. This morning, it dawned on me how yoga, and its gentle process, has gradually transformed me into a more authentic being, using a simple method of closing my eyes. Through his reminder over the years, I have been incorporating closing eyes while doing a pose whenever I can. Almost always, the minute I close my eyes, I'm immediately thrown off my balance. In trying to flow with it, keeping my balance, I exercise different muscles in my body. Slowly but surely, I learn to surrender, trusting my body to lead and my breathing to flow with the balance. I can feel the sensation, I can feel the peace, and I become more in tune with myself. As I embrace the experience of safe surrender with my morning yoga, peace gradually transitions with me into my everyday life. Suddenly, letting go becomes a part of life.

That's my biggest takeaway from yoga. Every day, I explore a new area of muscles I can strengthen, build and nurture, inside and outside of class. The practice allows me to build the trust to let go and explore the unknown. Trust was the biggest hurdle for me in the past, because my mom was taken away without warning, I didn't trust what I couldn't control. I demanded answers, confirmation from others. I pushed and patronized them to guarantee the outcome, and I didn't stop until I got it. This character had created bruises on those who were close to me. As the urge to control dims, serenity takes over, and I find myself enjoying silence. That's what yoga has helped me become. I'm now enjoying the melody of my breathing. "We can't determine the frequency of it," Kurt Johnsen said, "but we can certainly make sure the quality of it." How simple it is to be stress-free, and how amazingly beautiful and joyful it is to enjoy the simple things in life.

Early in the morning, when I'm sitting at my usual spot at home journaling -- doing my *Morning Pages*[15], I often feel so blessed about the morning. Just being here, seeing nature's smile get brighter as minutes turn into an hour, I'm building a passion for peaceful solitude. When I go hiking with friends, I can truly embrace the beauty of nature and feel so thankful I live so close to it. Even hiking in winter can bring so much joy; my steps exploring the soft path covered with snow, the trees with skinnier branches that wrap the paths, the wide open river that's temporarily frozen, the sound of winds and birds. I soak everything in, the music in nature. Every day, it's uniquely different, yet it offers the same peace and joy. This is what happiness is about. I can now feel it. Where was I before? In Indonesia, I hardly ever felt this way. I was moving from home to office, in and out of the car, from one place to another, brushing through life.

It's very humbling for me to take this path revisiting my past, peeling away the layers of life. At first, I only saw one area that seemed to be the reason I was stuck, as the layer was lifted, another one showed up underneath it. I must admit, I was, at times, wondering whether I should go deeper, whether I needed to keep peeling the layers. "Why wake up the sleeping lion?" I thought. I was anxious, reluctant, and apprehensive that my attempt would open old wounds. But at the same time I was curious. My wings were ready. I wanted to fly high. The only way I could do so freely was to let go of the pain that had compromised my growth. I remember a friend once shared Eleanor Roosevelt's phrase with me, and it went, "You gain strength, courage, and confidence by each experience in which you really stop to look fear in the face." I must do the thing I think I can't.

And I did. I gained the strength because of it. I made peace with the past, and because of it I have a different perspective about my past. I look at it through a different lens. Letting go falls into place, I don't have to try hard. When I realized it, the control had already gone. That's what I was experiencing during our trip to Pittsburg and beyond. Bit by bit the reve-lation emerged. Each time the new me showed up, I was caught by surprise at how I responded differently to things. Was that the first time, the first place I rediscovered myself? I can definitely say no, it wasn't. Looking back, I know it had started to happen a few years ago, but it wasn't as consistent, it wasn't as bright. I'm gratified I'm now here. It's now much easier to take a deep inhale of gratitude, and a long exhale of hope. I no longer see my shadow looking over my shoulder. I'm finally at the right moment and the right place in my life. Letting go of control has also allowed me to renew my relationship with three areas in my life I didn't know were a concern before:

FOOD AND HEALTH

I look at food and health from a different point of view now, a healthier one. My dad was diagnosed with Type-2 Diabetes at the age of sixty. My journey to help monitor his eating and lifestyle habits truly opened my eyes and mind about prevention and what we do with food -- our way of life around food. Dad took over a bakery business from his father, and expanded it to become an airport café and airline catering business. His life was around food. He explored it, learned it, experimented with it, and he enjoyed it. I remember I was shocked when I heard of his diagnosis, and gradually became upset about it. I couldn't come to terms with his inability to control his appetite. In my mind, I blamed him for not taking care of his health, until a nutritionist helped me understand how much his body had played tricks on him. "It's not that he couldn't control it. When the blood sugar level of a diabetic drops, his raging hunger can look ridiculous." That was my first intense encounter with the power of food. And then seven years later, my brother was struck by a mild stroke at the age of thirty-nine – work stress, smoking, lack of sleep and exercise. The idea of having two important people in my life facing health challenges was chilling for me. I didn't want to accept it. I decided to make health a priority and started to revisit the traditions my grandmother lived by decades ago. I reacquainted myself with the teaching, the lifestyle, the food I was brought up with. I started to control what I ate and I taught myself about health. I swallowed any information I considered good and beneficial to me. Armed with a controlling character that had been seasoned by life, you can imagine how I became around food and health. Strict rules of dos and don'ts, and I passed these along to those around me. I couldn't help but give comments on what my friends ordered when we ate out. I did the same to my dad, especially after his diagnosis. I became a food Nazi in my own home, particularly the first few years after I moved to Duluth. Charlie was initially a meat-and-potato kind of husband, and so was his son. He also had a quick-fix attitude to problems, reaching out for over-the-counter pills that easily ticked me off. I quickly took over ownership of the kitchen and grocery shopping. Fruits and vegetables were introduced into his life, water intake was increased, red meat was limited, coffee and butter were reduced, Cocoa Krispies were off the list, and sweets were almost banned.

I remember many instances when I was traveling without him, he would report what he ate to me when we talked on the phone. "You'd be proud of me, Sweetie. I had a full plate of greens and fish tonight." Other times, his sister would joke with me, "We had prime rib tonight, but we made sure Charlie didn't have too much of it, and just a little sliver of pie for dessert." I must say, the first five years after I was a part of his life, Charlie's health continued to improve, his annual physical was wonderful, and the doctor was happy. Most importantly, he felt much better, his prescriptions were reduced, allergy symptoms lessened, he bounces back faster from colds or flu, and he rarely gets sick. Although my intentions were good, to take control of his health, the way it was implemented could have been much more elegant.

Here's where IIN® has opened my mind. I learned that I could have been an orthorexia nervosa; one who was preoccupied with the notion of avoiding foods, maybe even activities, perceived to be unhealthy. I had induced stress into my family's life and mine. It was camouflaged with health and wellness. I remember, in Indonesia, how strict I was with food I loved yet considered not as healthy. I deprived myself from many delicacies I grew up with simply because they were too sweet, too much carbohydrates, too salty, et cetera. Or, it was fried, too oily, too much butter, there was always something wrong with it. I was playing tug-of-war with food. Pam Grout said it well in her book *E-Squared*, "When you feel guilty about consuming calories, your food picks up a negative vibe that ricochets right back at you."

Back in Indonesia, I often spent minutes in front of the counter at a bakery, contemplating whether I should buy something my grandmother used to make. Sometimes, after depriving myself from eating it, I binged on it, and then felt guilty or angry I had lost control of myself. Other times, I would go on a strict diet a few days after I indulged in rich food. When I had pizza, or my favorite Jakarta's signature noodles, I had lots of chili pepper to go with it so it could be flushed out of my system the next day. I didn't immediately reach for over-the-counter medicine when I had diarrhea until it was truly needed, because I lost weight with it. The risk I took to stay slim was dangerous, and my attempts to be in control of health were actually unhealthy. I have made more sense since I moved to Duluth. I have taken great strides toward holistic wellness. My experience and involvement with the mangosteen product has deepened my knowledge about health, and IIN® has completed the missing key to embracing wellness in its true and authentic sense.

Day by day, as our trip to Pittsburg, Kansas, was unfolding, I was surprised at how pleasant it was to let go. I didn't feel the urge to control what we did, rush to where we needed to go, definitely not on what we ate. As we were cruising the roads of Pittsburg and its surroundings -- gathering information and putting pieces of history into place for Charlie -- we often passed billboards of fried chicken restaurants. Huge and bold messages beckoned us to come in. The second time we passed it, we looked at each other and said, "What's up with Pittsburg and fried chicken?" The next day, when we saw another billboard about it, our curiosity was growing, "Looks like we're having fried chicken before we leave Pittsburg." And that evening, when we had dinner, we met a lovely couple, native to Pittsburg, who sat at a neighboring table. The husband was a retiree from a well-known chain of American department stores, who had traveled the country for forty years. He was their store merchandiser. During our visit we asked them what we shouldn't miss in Pittsburg. We, apparently, had gone to almost all the places they mentioned except the fried chicken restaurant. That sealed the deal. We decided we had to go and try this chicken the next day. They filled us in with the fried chicken history and its relevance to Pittsburg, "When you're here, at least try it once," they said.

That night, the thought of having unhealthy food crossed my mind. I have hardly eaten fried food since I moved to Duluth. Interestingly enough, I didn't dwell on it. I told Charlie, "I'm going to enjoy our vacation and get the feel of Pittsburg from its food, its people, and its land. I'm having fried chicken tomorrow, and I'm going to enjoy it." And his answer was,

"Good for you." So we did. With the help of the waitress we chose the original recipe and savored the fried chicken, mashed potato, German slaw, even cookies for dessert. Now we could officially claim that we'd been in Pittsburg. For the first time, in a very long time, I didn't feel guilty or upset after eating something unhealthy. It was a pleasant exploration while on a vacation, we enjoyed our night. And when our trip continued to Atlanta for Thanksgiving, spent at Charlie's brother and his family's home, we continued exploring the southern beauty through its food, its people, and its land.

The first day we were in Atlanta, we searched for Indonesian restaurants and decided to have Indonesian food for lunch. One of the places happened to be close to where my brother-in-law lived. His wife took us there and later accompanied us as we explored Atlanta. It was a buffet-style café; white rice or noodles, with two or three toppings. Charlie went ala carte. I couldn't decide which toppings I should go with. They all looked good and I wanted to try all of them. After lunch, we went to the Indonesian market next door, and I was giddy looking at so many spices, snacks, and foods that brought me back to Indonesia. I was going nuts, and every time I squeaked with excitement looking at an item or two, I heard Charlie agreeing, "You can have that, Sweetie."

I circled the aisles three times to make sure I had seen everything on the shelves while trying to decide what to buy. When I finally was back in front of the checkout counter to share my decision with Charlie, I saw many of the items had made it to the counter. Charlie gathered them based on the squeaks he heard when I saw them. As I was looking at them, I started weighing my selections. I returned some because I either could get them in our local grocery store, or I wouldn't use them as often. In the past, I would excessively buy things my eyes had missed for so long. I wanted to bring everything home, but they later ended up in the trash because most would pass the expiration date. The craving, and longing for things of my home country was more emotional than physical. The tendency to have more was because I hadn't only missed the food but more importantly, I was missing home, the people I hold dear in my heart, the memories of my upbringing, and the smell-look-touch-color of my grandmother's cooking. Everything seemed to have come to life when I saw the food in front of me. I wanted to have more of it so I could quench my thirst for home.

When we got home that evening, my sister-in-law shared what we had done during the day with her husband. And then she said something that helped me understand my relationship with food, especially Indonesian. "It was so interesting to watch you around foods from your home country, you were giddy and excited. You must have missed them a lot." By then, I had learned through IIN® about food craving; how we help our clients, and ourselves, to understand it, to find out what the underlying message is, what triggers it, and how to find healthier alternatives. It's the memory, the connections with my roots that I was missing. I do notice, when I'm stressed, I tend to crave rice, stir-fry foods, salty ones – things that remind me of home, Indonesia. I have a soft spot for potato chips sometimes. In Indonesia, I often had meals with our traditional crackers. When I moved to Duluth, I couldn't find them as easily. The closest cities to get them were St. Paul or Minneapolis where many Asians live, and they are 150 miles away. Potato chips were the closest substitute. Rice is one of Indonesian's staples. Most Indonesians won't consider having a meal unless there's rice with it. Many Indonesians will eat noodles on rice because noodles are considered topping -- just like Charlie still wants bread with any food. It's mind opening to learn the psychology of food. I'm enriched since I enrolled in IIN®. I continue becoming more aware of the messages my body is sending to me and how to handle them in a healthy way.

We continued on with our vacation exploring Savannah, Georgia, and Charleston, South Carolina after Atlanta. I was quite amazed to realize that many of southern foods reminded me of my home country; fried food – fish, chicken, seafood. Charlie and I enjoyed them all. We didn't go overboard, but we didn't deprive ourselves from enjoying them. And most importantly, I didn't punish myself, nor did I feel guilty from savoring them. Since then, I've embraced food unlike anything I had done in my life before. I wasn't lost in confusion. I enjoyed my food mindfully. My weight is stable. When I crave rice or nuts, or even potato chips because the stress of meeting a deadline, I let myself enjoy them. When I see my weight creep up a pound or two, I don't fuss. Sure enough, when the stress subsides, my hormones balance out, and my body lets go of the weight on its own.

It's amazing the revelation I gain when I let my body explore its journey. Letting go of control over food has built my body confidence. I trust it to make the right choices. I don't punish it when it wants to enjoy some treats. I let it play so it doesn't rebel and throw tantrums. Just like raising a child, when I have strict rules of dos and don'ts, I'm sending negative vibes that either make the child rebel, or follow directions like a robot. I want a smart child, who grows and explores life, not one who's jailed behind barbed-wires of dos and don'ts. I allow myself to be *bad* once in a while, especially when we're on vacation. That's the message I learned from Joshua Rosenthal, the Founder and Director of IIN®. I can be bad once in a while by having a treat. It's called a treat because I don't have it every day, otherwise, it'll be called food. When the body is given a chance to explore and enjoy, it knows when to stop. When I deprive my body from enjoying a treat, it'll binge somewhere, and I won't like how I feel afterward.

As I'm walking back food memory lane, I remember another philosophy I had around food. I was raised not to waste food. What I put on my plate, I should finish. Instead of putting lots on my plate that would end up wasted, I should start with small portions and have seconds later. I was always reminded of my fellow young children in Africa who couldn't eat. Somehow, that message was engrained deep in my mind. When I moved to Duluth and faced big American portions when we ate out, I would struggle to finish it. Boxing up leftover food after parts of it being forked and mixed or cut, didn't look as appetizing anymore to me. My solution now is to ask the waitress to bring a to-go box when she brings out the food. I divide it into two, immediately box half the portion and eat the other half. Most of the time, I can have two meals from one order. The challenge will be when I'm at a sit-down dinner party, finishing the whole plate will be too much, leaving the leftover on the plate is torture for me. Charlie doesn't mind stopping when he's full. I, on the other hand, feel guilty. I'm still working on *this* part of my relationship with food. Even if the food isn't as tasty, I have a challenge throwing food away. As a grand-daughter and daughter of bakers, I never witnessed food being thrown away in our household, unless it was stale because we didn't get to finish it soon enough, which was rare. I didn't learn about this relationship with food just from my grandfather and dad, but also from my mom's side of the family.

In the earlier years after I moved to Duluth, I would be tempted to put more on my plate because I liked the food, especially Indonesian food, or something that reminded me of home. "If I didn't have enough right here and now, when would be the chance for me to have it again?" It's silly to hear me say it now, as if that was the only chance I could have such a dish, as if that's the end of it, I couldn't find more of it in the future. It was a challenge to let go of something I liked or loved. I wanted to have more of it and hold on to it longer. The feeling of not having enough was rooted deep in my childhood; not having enough of my mom, of my dad – I had to wait to share stories, or ask for something, wait until there came a time for him to visit my brother and me. It's amazing how one particular event in the past can follow one's life for decades. I've always been curious about the effect of someone's upbringing to his or her later life. I was curious, and possibly suspicious, about my own.

I've since learned to treat my body with love; listen to it, respect it, and take care of it. I want to explore life and live it to the fullest. This body of mine is the only vehicle that will take me to the future, accompany me on my exploration till the end of my journey. I can't trade this body in. I can't sell it. I can't buy a new one. So, I will take good care of it. I open a two-way loving communication with it, daily. I thank my body for sending me messages I need to hear, for responding to me. I thank the food I'm having. I trust it will nourish me. I let it bring great energy to me – for my body, my mind and my soul, so I'll grow well and healthy, strong and happy. I dance with food in harmony. I partner with it, and I appreciate what I have. Life is good!

MONEY

I was raised around entrepreneurs. My grandfathers, from both sides of the family, were business owners, so was my dad. I've always been drawn to entrepreneurship since I was young.

I sold custom jewelry when I was in college to make extra pocket money, which I continued doing during my earlier years in advertising. I was also selling clothes to colleagues. They paid in two or three installments. I would get free new clothing every time I sold three or four dresses. I loved it. My family wasn't rich, but we had more than enough to live and enjoy. I'm forever grateful for what I had.

Money, especially on my maternal side of the family was handled with care. We were kind of secretive about it, almost never talked about it. It was treated as one of our valuables. We didn't flaunt it. We didn't gamble with it. We didn't discuss it except when necessary, and usually with a different tone of voice. Growing up, I somehow got the feeling that talking about it was like sending a message that we were either greedy or showing off, as if that was the only important thing in life. We witnessed how money ruined those we knew, so we subconsciously built a notion that money couldn't buy happiness. I was one of those people who thought money was a necessary evil – can't live without it, but can't guarantee happiness with it either. Growing up, I was frequently reminded about it, not so much verbally, but through actions and examples. The grownups around me seemed to know when to insert the reminder as we talked or witnessed incidents that had happened. For instance, when a relative fell deep into debt because of overspending on unnecessary things, or got enrolled in the world of materialism, one popular reminder I'd hear was, "That's what money can do to you." And, it would be delivered with a voice of disapproval, or, *see what I mean* kind of tone. Other times, when we heard a family going through a nasty separation, I would hear, "Remember, money can't buy happiness." The tone of voice would send a vibe that translated in my mind as money creates problems. Without realizing it, I carried the thought with me and subconsciously reminded myself to keep a distance from it. "I should be grateful for what I have. Keep what's needed, just enough." Having money was considered fate, or a factor of luck, and it could be testing.

My dad, on the other hand, never had the need to remind my brother and me of money. He never talked about it, nor shared his struggle with us either. I know most parents don't want to bother their children with money, but in dad's case, it's because he wanted to insulate us from any struggle after we lost our mom. As a result, my brother and I never knew of any struggle he may have had, money related or otherwise. We just didn't touch the subject. I remember when I graduated from high school, it was the first year where the five major colleges in Indonesia had a collective admission test for high-school graduates. I wasn't accepted at either of the two major colleges I applied. After a family discussion, we agreed that I should move to Jakarta, where my brother was already living and going to college. I entered a tutoring program to help get me prepared for the next year's test. We also agreed I should apply to more colleges because two might not be enough. During that year, I was toying with the idea of pursuing higher education in America instead. After some personal contemplation, I shared the idea with my dad. It was around the same time I received notices I was accepted to three colleges.

Dad had always been very wise in responding to a request. His reasoning had always made sense to me. It was always logical, I would find it difficult to plea or beg. Even if I was disappointed, it wouldn't last long. "A hundred thousand students compete to get a spot in these great colleges, only 10% are accepted, and you're one of them. You knew how difficult it was to get in. If you take this on, and once you graduate, if you still want to pursue a degree in America, we'll find a way."

Wasn't that logical? The college I was accepted to was, and I believe still is, considered one of Indonesia's Ivy League. Why would I brush off such an opportunity? That one seat would be wasted if I ditched it, one seat someone else could have benefitted from. Later in life I found out, money was tight for dad during that time. He had two older children in college, and needed to plan for the future education of the children he had with his new wife.

Another example of not talking about money is I never negotiated my salary, never fought for it. I remember the first time I started earning a salary. I was just happy and grateful I was hired, and my dad reminded me of tithing. As I moved up the ladder in my career, I never countered the offer I was presented. My dad raised me to be a good worker, show my best, and people would appreciate me. Even though he never worked for somebody other than his own father, he was a disciplined person and businessman. I recall our conversation when I told him I was hired at my first job. "I'm proud of you. Work honestly and respectfully, show them you're valuable," he said. If I ever was disappointed or felling unappreciated, he would say, "They'll come around. Do good. You'll be noticed." So I never asked. He taught me to be tenacious in life, and to appreciate what I did and had. "You can be a sweeper for all we care, but if you do your job well, you'll be the best sweeper." When we returned to our hometown during school break, he fondly reminded my brother and me of the story of *Jan,* a man who had worked for my grandfather since my dad was young, and stayed working for dad until he retired.

Jan was a quiet young man, a persistent and hard working one. After everyone else had gone home, my grandfather often saw Jan still working, finishing a project he had started that day. He wasn't a 9-to-5 kind of person. He wasn't bothered by overtime, and he'd stay to finish a task. My grandfather was appreciative of that attitude. When dad took over the bakery business from his father, Jan continued working for dad. When he reached the end of his tenure, after working for the family for more than forty years, dad suggested that he retire. But Jan kept coming back to work every day. He said he'd die of boredom if he couldn't work, so dad took him back and gave him projects daily. Jan never asked for a salary, he was just happy to be useful. He was a jack-of-all-trades. Because of this attitude my grandfather valued him, and so did dad. He took care of Jan and gave him a retirement package when he finally couldn't work anymore. Dad believed people would notice the result of a loyal and consistent worker and would value that person accordingly.

Another instance is about giving. Whether it's to a family member, a relative who was in need, or general donation for a certain cause, my dad hardly ever wanted his name to appear on the list. The more anonymous it was, the fewer people who knew, the better. He strove for anonymous giving. His belief was, "If you truly want to help, your name shouldn't be there, or anywhere. When it comes sincerely from your heart, you should be out of the picture. Question your sincerity before someone else does." I took this one to heart, and sub-consciously the unspoken teaching about money as well. When I was living in Surabaya, I had to wait until my dad came to visit to go shopping and buy things I wanted. I don't think I ever asked Mam for money unless it was related to school. I didn't want to rock the boat when I could sense that money wasn't a luxury. Mam had to work hard to support many people under her roof. Because it was beyond my control when money would be available, I held on to it as long as I could when I had it. My modus operandi was to be careful and strict with my spending.

I was afraid of not having enough. I was running on the fuel of scarcity rather than abundance. On several occasions, especially during the delicate times of closing down our furniture business, the tighter I was with money, the faster it seemed to leave us. I must have choked it to death. I can still relate to the stress that came with having such feeling of scarcity.

In some instances in life, I felt conflicted if I had to ask for money in exchange for my service. Or even when I fought for my right, I would feel guilty afterward. I often failed to appreciate myself. I didn't have as much difficulty negotiating or discussing money when I was building a career representing an employer. I somehow had that separation, I needed to fight for what I thought was appropriate for a business or organization. But when it came to me, my own business, and my own service, I somehow felt I always overcharged others. Lots of thoughts would dance in my brain. *What if they can't afford it? Should I give it for free? She really needs it. What if I help just the one who needs it the most?* In front of those prospective clients or customers, I then appeared to have conflicting messages. While having a debate about money in my mind, I was sending the vibe that was picked up as being unassertive and incapable. They might not be able to pinpoint exactly what, but they could feel it. I'm just wondering how much I had sabotaged my own success because of that, because I wasn't comfortable or confident talking about money. My brain was often running on a non-profit mode. I would easily feel uncomfortable or guilty as if I took advantage of someone who was in need. A few times, I was instead, taken advantage of by some people. Interestingly enough, I would get upset at myself. I felt it was my fault, I was too trusting and wasn't savvy enough.

It took me a while to understand and dig deeper into this

part of my past about money. This, I must say, was the most difficult one to let go. It was pushed so deep in my being and it was so subtle, we hardly ever talked about it. It wasn't linked to any traumatic event either, so I couldn't identify the source of the problem. It's challenging to let go of something I can't put my finger on. It didn't help when I realized that a lot of people felt the same. Consequently, I thought that was what money was all about, the necessary evil. As soon as I witnessed or experienced unfortunate incidents regarding money, I was reminded what money could do.

I started looking at money differently when I got involved in network marketing. This industry, its leaders and people that run the business, were and still are, the ones who have helped me shift my mind about money. At one of its events, a minister was speaking. He wasn't only a minister, but also a motivational speaker, as well as a businessman -- he had four businesses. He, quoting a verse in the Bible, said, "It isn't what we have that's evil, it's what we love." He continued on saying, "We can have as much money as we want. God wants us to be prosperous, to be rich, and in abundance, so we can be generous." He loves cheerful givers. Imagine what the gift can become when we give generously and sincerely because we want to, not because we have to, the gift will expand abundantly. Cheerful givers will attract cheerful receivers. And the cheerful cycle goes around.

So where did I get the idea that money was evil? I don't think my family intentionally wanted me to have this perception about money, that was how I perceived it, based on what I saw, heard, experienced and learned. It's unfortunate that bad things seem to be happening to bad people. It isn't money that's bad, it's what we do with it. I remember listening to Jim Rohn talk about this matter in his teaching audio, "Money is a form of energy that tends to make us more of who we already are." If one, by nature, is happy, he'll be happier. If one is giving, she'll be more giving. If one is a cheater, an addict, or lazy then one will become more of those as well. A few books were introduced to me through my journey with network marketing. They helped me slowly shift my perspective toward money. Once I saw money from a different point of view, and outwitted the idea of evil, I slowly was able to move on and create new experiences with it. Letting go of old perceptions requires effort and reminders through continuous learning. This one is a work-in-progress for me. I have crossed many bridges since, I've taken consistent strides forward, and I can feel my perspective toward money has gradually become healthier.

I'm building momentum. I've created a new partnership with money. It's very interesting to realize that once my mind is moving toward abundance instead of scarcity, I receive validation. I don't anymore hear as much bugging chatter in my head saying, "What if it runs out? What if it is stolen? What if someone cheats me?" Instead, I can be at peace and know that the Universe will provide a way to solve any challenge I have with money, and it sure does. I learn to let go and surrender to a higher energy. And this trust has tremendously helped me move on with peace and confidence.

MY HIGHER POWER

I was raised a Catholic. I was baptized a few days after I was born. My brother and I went to Catholic schools. We went to church every Sunday with the grownups in our life. As adults, we almost never ditched Sunday mass either, it's been internalized. We grew up in a small town and we knew every home on our street, and its owners. Growing up, I never felt discriminated against because of my faith, even though

Indonesia is the largest Moslem population in the world. The majority of my friends, consequently, were Moslem. I even dated a few in my life. In the first seven years of my life, my brother and I were friends with a neighboring family who had eight children, whose middle children were about our ages. We respected them as they observed the fasting month, and joined them in a celebration of Eid al-Fitr. We helped them decorate their home to welcome the big day. They respected us when we observed Lenten season and celebrated our holidays with us. We remained friends until we all left this small hometown and reconnected when we lived in Jakarta.

I practiced my faith. Some might think I was a devout Catholic. All the grownups around me were my examples, so I adopted them as part of my upbringing. When I was in my teens, I started to become more aware of the different religions around me. In Indonesia, we have lots of public holidays based on Hindu, Buddhism, Christianity, and Islam. I'm proud I was raised in a country that respects diversity. We need to, with the many subcultures and customs we have. We're enriched by respecting each other's assets. As a Catholic who was brought up according to its principles, I followed the rituals. My faith raised me to be faithful, I didn't know any other way. I built a relationship with God by learning and following his teaching, and emulating what my parents did. Over time, it became automatic. I know now how fixating routine can be. Prior to getting entangled in the cycle of work, I was hypnotized by the routine of practicing my faith. Prayer was recited automatically just as getting up and going to sleep. Then slowly, going to church was becoming an automatic activity as well, and my relationship with God was on cruise control. I hardly ever opened a Bible, let alone read it. I knew the content of certain verses and could paraphrase them, but couldn't recall which disciple said which one. My family was private Catholics, I always considered I was too. We didn't go to church or practiced our faith loudly, literally and figuratively. We did it as our way to communicate with God. That's how I perceived and believed it.

I was born a Catholic because my parents were, our family was, and our way of living reflected that teaching. We observed privately. The concept of being faithful was engrained in me. I was a faithful confession goer, although as a teen, I debated which sin worth asking for penance and which one could get a green light. I didn't want to bore the priest with the same sin every week. When the church introduced the idea of a communal reconciliation service, I was relieved because I didn't have to pour out my sins in front of someone I know. Many times I went to a different church just so I didn't have to whisper to a familiar face.

I was though, at certain points in my life, experiencing times of discernment, asking my heart what it meant to be a Catholic. Through life, especially during trying times, or when I needed something big and important, I would usually increase my frequency of praying; before an exam, a long journey, or while making a big decision. I sometimes chuckled seeing people at early morning mass, who I suspected were the non-regulars. They must have something big to go through, just like me. I had treated God, and my faith, as a bumper, a life vest. I put it on when I needed it, and would forget when wishes were granted. Every now and then, I would get disappointed when things didn't go my way. At times, my tone of prayer was anger. I demanded God to fulfill what I thought I really needed. Other times, I appeared as a beggar. I played victim, I was needy. That's what my routine had made me become, the concept of relationship and partnership was blurry. It's like a refrigerator. I stuff things into it, pull things out when I need it. It stays plugged in all the time to guarantee electricity running continuously. It's functional, it's a working fridge, but I go to it *only* when I need something. I treated God like a thing. It was disrespectful. What came out of my mouth wasn't in harmony with what I did.

I practiced my faith because it was part of my upbringing. I wasn't a practicing Catholic by choice, it was a given. Growing up, I was afraid if I acted against what I was taught, I'd be a sinner. When I was in my twenties, I was asked by a close friend, who happened to be Catholic, to accompany her to a fortune teller. We were discussing this issue a few times prior to going, lots of questions running back and forth between us. "Do we disrespect God by trusting a human being to tell our future? Does this person know it all, better than God? Is it possible that God uses this person to bridge and verbalize his message to us? After all, psychics seemed to be vibrating on a different frequency than normal people, perhaps they sense something we don't." Yet the thought of crossing the line was bugging me. When I finally accompanied her to the fortune teller, I had a reading as well. I felt guilty afterward, the feeling lingered for a while, and it haunted me. I was also one of those Catholics who felt guilty if I missed church and communion on Sunday, if I failed the Ten Commandments. I had a lot of sins growing up, and I dreaded admitting my sins in a confession.

A few years ago, I was visiting with a friend, who was going through a separation with her husband of twenty years. She was adopting Christianity, going to a Bible study, and seriously considering converting. During that visit, she made a comment, or perhaps it was more of a question, "Why does God allow despair in one's life? Why does He allow wars or children to be killed, and abandoned?" I answered the way most people would, and I believed in this answer as well, "God allows it to happen so we can learn from it." She pushed forward, "But why would God use children, the innocents, to make adults learn? Doesn't God love children? Why use innocent children who still have life to live? How could He let life be snatched away from them?" I couldn't answer these follow-up questions. For a while, they hung in my mind as well. Why God?

Then one day, I found the answer in a church bulletin. The priest said it was related to freedom. In essence, this is what he said, "God allows us to do evil because if He stopped us from doing it, we would no longer have our freedom. And the benefit of having free will outweighs all the bad side effects of free will. Our inability to understand suffering is part of our inability to understand God himself. If we do, then He really wouldn't be God at all. When all is said and done, probably the full explanation of all this is beyond us. The easiest and most honest answer to this is – we just don't know." That, I thought, was what letting go is all about. Letting God, the Universe, or the Higher Power take over. That's what Pam Grout wanted me to experience through the experiments she shared in her book *E-Squared*. Ask, and claim the result, just don't meddle in the how it gets to you.

I had been chasing answers throughout life. I wanted confirmation. I often wasn't satisfied with what I got or what was given to me especially when it wasn't what I had in mind. I became upset and demanding, "Why?" It was tiring being a nonstop runner, I didn't have a home. At times, I would easily get swayed by winds of opinions and arguments between people because I didn't have a steady ground. When something happened to the institution of my religion, I felt embarrassed, or responsible. When people were busy chiming and condemning, I felt it was directed to me as its follower. It was difficult to separate me from them because the reason I was here, my purpose, was blurry. Other times, I would be dancing between two terms, two labels; do I consider myself a spiritual being or a religious one? Does it have to be either or? Why can't it be both?

When I started searching and eventually embarked on a journey within, one by one the magical keys that eventually transformed my life were introduced to me. I became more aware of life. I finally got in touch with me. I slowly surrendered and let go of the control that bound me for decades. That's when peace finally resided permanently in me. I grew up spiritually. I can now see and feel the answer from my Higher Power. I can feel it from talking to someone, listening to or reading something. He does talk to me in different ways, I have no doubt. I can surrender and know that the answer will present itself. I no longer do things because I'm afraid of the consequences, or punishment, when I don't do it. I do it because I want to. I no longer demand, shove, and disrespect God, the Universe, or my Higher Power. I open a bridge that's functional 24/7. Once I embrace and understand this, and most importantly feel it, my relationship with God grows, and I'm also growing as a person. I was brought up a Catholic, I still am a Catholic. But most importantly, now I'm a person who feels there is divine power around me. I can tap into it. I can reach out to it. It's open 24/7.

When my mind is breathing peace, and it isn't crowded by unnecessary thoughts and doubts, I can see and think clearly. I've become more tolerant. Instead of reacting to things, especially uncomfortable things, I respond. I can turn off the television, I can move away from bad energy that tries to enroll me in, I can stay away from complaining chatter around me. And I learn to accept people even when I can't accept their actions. It's like being a part of a family. I'm just one of many. When one of my siblings did something bad, or evil, I felt the pain in my family. Our parents raised us all the same. They taught and reminded us to do well, to respect and love others. But there seems to always be a black sheep or two within a family, an adult who's free to do his own thing. He may land on the wrong foot, end up in the wrong environment, or with the wrong people. Does the action of this sibling make the parents, the family, bad? Absolutely not. Does his action cause pain within the family? Of course it does. As much as we regret or may condemn what happened, we can't be responsible for it. I've been more aware not to get on the band wagon when similar things happen to other families. I used to dig into it, talk about it, condemn it. What did it do to me? It amplified the frustration, it stayed with me. The more I talked about it, the more upset I became, for no reason, and later, I took it out on other things in my life. It wasn't worth it.

The human mind is the most intelligent computer, if we allow it to be. If we provide the environment for it to be so, it can create abundantly. When my body feels better, my mind is healthier, and my soul sings lovelier. Letting go of clutter, pollution, and toxin in the mind requires action. At first, I didn't know that what I was doing was right, but I could feel something was pulling me forward. I went with the flow, it felt right. Jim Rohn's wisdom continued beaming into my mind, "Your life doesn't get better by chance, it gets better by change." I need to be willing to let change come into my life. Having an inquisitive mind is great: ask, discuss, brainstorm, learn and grow.

My role as an active participant of life is to continue spreading love, peace and joy. I keep reminding myself to do so because I want to, not because I have to. God, the Universe, my Higher Power is a generous, loving, abundant, and accommodating energy. I don't anymore have thoughts that deceive. I can single-mindedly send my intention and know that the answer will be available. I open a two-way communication with my Higher Power, I talk to him -- anytime, anywhere. I used to refer to this as praying. My prayer is serious at times, but it can also be lively and humorous. God is a humorous energy. It's very liberating to surrender to the unknown, yet know for sure the answer will show up. I've renewed my relationship with my faith. You can call me a born-again participant of life, especially my own. That's another takeaway I gain from this journey within.

SETTING INTENTIONS

By now, I have seen enough evidence about trusting my intentions. I stop entertaining self-doubt chatter, or at least I'm more aware when it starts showing up. *E-Squared* has helped me realize how loving, generous, and accommodating the Universe is. Since reading this book, and experiencing the revelation I had with the author's first experiment, my con-fidence has slowly been restored.

I was fortunate my colleague introduced me to AsiaWorks. I know I was feeling unsettled at that time. I remember thinking, "OK, your five-year mark is almost up!" By then, I was aware of a pattern that showed up toward the end of a five-year cycle in my career, I would start feeling restless, itchy to move on. I was on my third cycle of five years when I joined AsiaWorks. When I was at the leadership stage of the program, I had to set goals, and one of them was related to personal life, specifically, meeting someone. I was resisting the process because I didn't think I needed to push myself to find someone. I was happy where I was -- so I thought. Looking back, I could see why I felt that way. I was just drifting with the current, I was too lazy to think that I had to make an effort to meet someone. Comfort had made me numb. "Naaah, I don't need it," I rationalized. I often had a feeling of nah, blah, or 'whatever' then. Yet, the small group of friends in the program, especially my two buddies, were gung-ho about exploring. "Come on, get out there," they said, "Do the unusual, surprise yourself." They suggested I look into personal-column method of meeting people. "Never," I said convincingly. "I don't want to be stalked by strangers. There are lots of crazy people out there," I rationalized again. It made sense, I thought. But this gung-ho group of idea-churning people wouldn't give up. It wasn't about meeting someone, they said, "It's about pushing yourself to get out there, out of your comfort zone, trying something you have never done before. Most importantly, learning about *you* in the process."

Reminiscing on that lengthy discussion with my group, Kurt Johnsen's voice, my virtual yoga teacher, suddenly comes to mind. During a morning rendezvous with yoga, as I was standing on one leg, I heard him say, "When you're thinking instead of feeling the sensation from the pose, I have a solution for you." I was immediately brought back to reality. My mind started to fly away just seconds ago, that's how easy it was to drift into la-la land. "Raise your hands and open up," Johnsen suggested. He always offered us three to four options to do a pose based on the challenge level. "Not enough sensation? Look up." I was amazed at how timely his remarks always are, as if he saw me day-dreaming. "I bet your leg starts shaking," he added, "That's how your muscles grow." Then he challenged us to go further, "Still easy? I can fix that, close your eyes, explore."

Every day, Johnsen elegantly inserts some wisdom through his instructions as I glide from one pose to another. Not only that I experience the benefits of yoga for my health from an hour-long of meditation, but my mind is also enriched by the wisdom he shares as I'm dancing through the music of my breathing. At the beginning of my encounter with yoga, I thought I would just learn and gain flexibility. Six years later, I fully embrace the gift yoga has brought into my life. Yoga has prepared me to go underground, explore the deep within. It continues to train me to get in tune with my feelings. The sensations from the poses I do each morning, eventually move outside of the class, unto the stage of life. I'm grateful I have found this valuable practice. When I'm drifting away, hearing my thoughts, and chatter in my mind, I don't live in the presence. I'm not here. Being comfortable doing a pose isn't the goal, I need to expand, explore the same pose in a more challenging way. "That's the only way you'll grow," Johnsen says. Otherwise, my muscles will easily get used to that comfortable position and they get complacent. What benefit will I gain if I don't grow? Isn't that so relevant to life? Now the idea of 'getting out of a comfort zone' makes more sense to me.

Yoga guides and empowers me to practice exploring the unfamiliarity of life, embracing and enjoying it. "This is proof that peace comes from within. It doesn't matter what you're doing, what happens around you, you'll stay calm in the present," Johnsen confirms. And slowly, that calm response branches into real life. I was too familiar with what I was doing back then, in life and at work. I started to get bored because I was basically going in circles, on life's baggage carousel. It was true I had different clients and brands to work with while I was involved in advertising, but what I did was basically the same. I went to work, came home, taking the same route, Monday through Friday. Come Saturday, I would indulge in pampering body treatments and going to movies, then spending time with my niece and nephew on Sunday. As soon as the week ended,

Monday showed up again. Everything became familiar, and felt familiar. It was like eating the same food day in and day out. I couldn't taste the individuality of the ingredients anymore, everything was blah because it was predictable. Nothing much to learn when I was already so familiar with everything. I was hypnotized by routine.

When my experience with AsiaWorks pushed me to stretch my possibilities, I was hesitating, it wasn't easy to explore the unfamiliar. But at the same time I was also curious. My buddies suggested that I explore the internet to meet people, "Find people outside of Indonesia so you aren't obligated to meet them, and they can't stalk you." I thought it was an idea worth exploring. After all, I stepped out of my comfort zone when I was at the mall a few months earlier, finally met the sisters, and took them to lunch. "Let's explore some more of life," I thought. I finally landed on a website and developed a friendship through email with six pen-pals; one each in Sydney, Australia, Johannesburg, South Africa, Germany, Hongkong, and two were in the United States. I met with the last two who lived on opposite coasts in the United States during my end-of-the-year vacation in the country. Nice men, no connection though. I came back from my vacation and shared my experience with the group. By then, our program had ended. I shared the highlight of my experience with them, and then concluded, "I'll now go back to my normal life, to my usual way of meeting people." I did, though, feel proud of myself to have gone out of my familiar way to experience life – to run the risk of being embarrassed, feeling out of place, and disappointed. I applauded myself for being brave to try it. It was worth trying, at least one time.

A week after I returned from my vacation, I went back to the dating website and terminated my membership. Interestingly enough, a week later, an email showed up from someone in

Minnesota. A nice one page email, respectfully written, explaining the person's plan to vacation in Indonesia, specifically the island of Bali. He was traveling with his friend and they had never been to our part of the world before. He thought he would do some initial research, and hopefully meet someone in Indonesia who could introduce that part of the country to them; suggest what to explore, where to go, what to avoid, and so on. That person was Charlie. I entertained him with some ideas, shared information with him, answered his questions, and suggested what not to miss while in Bali. By then, we had been exchanging emails for about two, three days, and my curiosity was about to explode, so I asked him, "How did you find me? How did you get my email address?"

Charlie didn't know how it happened, but later we figured it could have been something to do with the way he did his research online. He kept clicking on a link that looked interesting, and consequently, he jumped from one site to another and finally landed on the online-dating website. He scrolled up and down and realized he could see profiles and pictures of women from around the world. He then looked for Indonesia, and his eyes brought him to my picture. Much later into our marriage, he mentioned the reason why my picture stood out. He said because I was the one with a non-glamorous profile picture. Armed with what I learned from how he found me, I sent another email to the online-dating website and explained what had happened. The customer service staff response was, "You terminated your membership in the middle of the month, you had already been charged for the month's membership fee, we thought you should enjoy what you already paid." Nice, but I wasn't expecting anymore emails. They assured me my profile would be taken off the site.

A month after that first email, Charlie arrived in Bali with his friend, on Valentine's Day. A few days before he left Duluth, he realized that I didn't live on Bali. I lived an hour and a half away, by plane, in Indonesia's capital, Jakarta. Charlie was trying to find ways to fly to Jakarta, but of course, he couldn't find reasonable tickets in Duluth for traveling within Indonesia's cities. At first, I didn't make any promises to meet him in person, until it was his last weekend in Bali. I found fairly reasonable round-trip tickets for a weekend in Bali so I flew out to meet him. We spent the whole Saturday exploring Bali. We had a very nice time and good conversations, but no romantic connection. Nevertheless, it was a pleasant visit. We exchanged business cards, agreed to keep in touch, and I flew back to Jakarta on Sunday. Three months after his Bali visit, I was on a business trip to Chicago for ten days, we reconnected, and the bridge to Duluth started to develop.

Was it fate? Was the momentum to step out of my familiar zone building? Or was it something else? As I'm writing this book, and reminiscing on my first experiment with Pam Grout's *E-Squared*, I suddenly remember a moment in New York City, at a Christmas Eve mass. I remember having a heart-to-heart dialogue with my Higher Power, and made a deal, "If there's someone out there for me, do lead him to me. But if there isn't, help me truly enjoy my life to the fullest -- not worrying about family's concern, or what others think of my being single." That's all I asked.

I was born and raised in a culture where society seemed to have predicted my life. Once I finished college, the most common question that came my way would be, "Do you have a boyfriend?" This would then be followed by, "When are you going to get married?" If I got married, the next most popular tune I'd hear would be, "When are you going to have a baby?" -- you get the idea. Decades have since passed and nothing much has changed. Baby girls are still born, they go to school, get a job (this is a new addition to the cycle), get married, have babies, raise a family, juggle work, family, life. Then work hard to send their children through the same cycle, retire, babysit grandchildren, grow old and die. Interestingly enough, this was not just a cycle of women's life around me, it was everybody's cycle of life, it didn't matter what the culture, or gender was. We expected the same from ourselves. Not to follow the script of life was out of the ordinary, coloring outside of the line meant something must be wrong.

I was one of the rebels. I was fortunate my immediate family didn't pressure me to get married young. But for twenty years, I was bombarded by a broken record from society and distant relatives. At a few points in my life, I thought something *was* wrong with me – maybe I was choosy, I was demanding, I was controlling. It got the best of me. I became more cynical and sarcastic with my answers when they asked me. Was it wrong what those who followed this cycle of life did? Of course it wasn't. But I shouldn't just follow the crowd simply because everyone was heading in that direction. Just because most people married didn't mean I should. That was the point of my dialogue with somebody from the Upper Room that Christmas Eve. I wanted a life I would enjoy. And then I surrendered to the Universe, I wasn't going to dwell on *how*. "Please, just give me a sign, whichever way that's mine." I was honestly relieved after that. I enjoyed the rest of my vacation, and New Year in New York City. I came back to work refreshed. Three weeks after that solemn night at church, Charlie's email showed up in my inbox. And fifteen months later, I landed in Duluth, Minnesota. That was the start of a new beginning for me. I stepped out of my familiar zone and stretched myself beyond anything I had done before. I learned about me, and that was what brought me here. When I did finally come across Pam Grout's *E-Squared*, I received validation. I got a confirmation I was on the right track. I had doubted myself often in the past, I discounted my potential, and ended up sabotaging my success.

The first time I went to New York City was for my sabbatical year, in 1990. At that time, I also wanted to explore the possibility of going to school, getting a degree in journalism. I had always loved writing, I considered myself analytical and curious, so I took some courses that might be beneficial to me when I applied to a journalism program; creative writing, personal essay, public speaking. With an endorsement from one of the teachers, I had an interview with a gentleman from the admissions office. His response was discouraging but certainly didn't defeat me. He suggested that I apply to a different program before going into journalism, simply because English was my second language. He didn't think I would be able keep up with the journalism courses. "You need to breathe, dream, and think in English." Those were his words.

A few years after I returned to Indonesia and reentered the advertising industry, some friends suggested that I write a book about copywriting, for those who were considering this career. There were two things I've always wanted to do since I was in middle school, write a book, and a movie. So when some friends suggested a book on copywriting, I entertained the idea for a while, but I couldn't come up with a topic I was game to do. Many decades have passed since the idea was first launched. I'm now writing my first book, in a language that's not my mother tongue. The language I didn't breathe, dream, and think in until I moved to this country. I didn't embrace the idea of setting intentions then, I didn't know the power of setting one, and claiming it. Here I am now, forty years after I first launched the thought about it in Middle School, twenty-five years after I was discouraged from applying to the New York University Journalism Program, thirteen years after I rode on the momentum to explore a new life in a new country, but only less than two years after I read and embraced the concept of setting intentions introduced by Pam Grout. I'm here writing my first book, in English.

Someone in network marketing once shared a story with me, which many have quoted, I don't know who told it first. I guess the who isn't important, the story did get me thinking then, and since. "There are three birds sitting on a fence, and two decided to fly off. How many are still left on the fence?" he asked. I knew it was a trick question, most of us would probably say one. I did too. One was the immediate response that came to mind. The answer is *still* three birds. The two creatures were only deciding to fly, but never actually did. They could talk and plan all day, but until they let go of their grip and pushed themselves to take off, they'd be still sitting on that fence until death came to peel life from them. It takes momentum to fly high, but it takes that first step, the first jump – the one we argue and reason about in our minds -- to lift us up. In the past, I often experienced this going back-and-forth in my mind. I declared my intention but almost immediately after that I stepped back. I created many logical excuses why I shouldn't do it. I sent many conflicting messages to the Universe. No wonder nothing came to fruition. Self-doubt is the most subtle deceiving energy. I have let go of self-doubt that has hand-cuffed me for most of my life. I'm declaring my intentions to the Universe. I'm ready to fly even higher. Now the sky is truly the limit.

I made peace with my past and let go of temptations to control and to be perfect. I can now see the road ahead more clearly, and I can feel the sensation of being one with my purpose of getting there, achieving what I set my mind to. Do I still have doubts? Absolutely. I'm not the all-time positive thinker, but I'm now more aware of it, so I can deal with it before it takes me hostage.

WINGS TO FLY

We said goodbye to Charleston, South Carolina, on a foggy Thursday morning. We put 17,000+ steps the day before, according to my Fitbit, circling Charleston's Historic District – in and out of old churches, cemeteries, parks, and shops. We went all the way to the end of the South of Board, we explored the French Quarter, the Museum Mile, then enjoyed southern dishes at Hyman's Seafood for dinner – crispy flounder, collard greens, grits, coleslaw, and all that jazz. I can still smell the crispy fish, fresh from the kitchen, its sizzling sound becoming more erratic as it reached our table. It reminded me of Indonesian home-cooking – fish and Indonesian *sambal*[16] on warm rice, ate by hand. It surely was *finger lickin' good*. Charlie and I loved the south, we wished we could stay longer, "A reason to come back," we told ourselves. We decided to drive as far north as we could in one day since the weather channel had mentioned the Midwest could be snowy and slippery that weekend.

After twelve hours of straight driving, we stopped and stayed in a hotel just north of Chicago. We were glad we didn't have to deal with the traffic of the metropolitan area the next day. We walked into our home on Friday afternoon, tired but happy. "I truly enjoyed our vacation," I said to Charlie, "It was really pleasant. I can't remember feeling this way with our previous vacations." He looked at me with questioning eyes, "Why do you think that is?" I thought for a second and said, "I guess I wasn't uptight, I was relaxed and curious to explore." I don't know whether he knew what it meant for me to say that. I'm not sure whether he saw and felt the difference between this vacation and the previous ones we were on. It had been a while since our last long vacation together, but I don't need to dwell on why. I, for one, was refreshed and ready to embark on a new journey. Right before we left for Pittsburg, IIN® had extended an invitation to me, in addition to the school program, to get on with another program -- writing and self-publishing a book. I said yes to it.

My initial thought was to write a book as part of launching a health coaching business after I graduated from IIN®. These past ten months alone have been an eye and mind opening experience for me. This experiential program with IIN® has renovated my thinking, my knowing, and my doing in relation to food. And suddenly, the last key to the combination of life was presented to me. This finally propelled me to fly high with bursts of intentions. It was truly a grand bonus. When I started with IIN®, my intention was to take a journey within, to understand myself around food, and my body's relationship with food. Through every module I listened to and implemented, Joshua Rosenthal and the crew at IIN® reminded me often, "Check back with your intention. Are you still on track with it? Is it expanding?" Halfway through the program, his reminder becoming a forward pull for me, "See your intention beyond IIN®. What do you see yourself becoming after you graduate, beyond the certification?" This was truly an intriguing question. It made me stop and think, it certainly pulled me forward to see the many possibilities I hadn't thought before.

I started visiting my life's purpose, seeing how far I can fly beyond IIN®. My wings are stronger and wider now. I embarked on a health-coaching journey to connect and partner with the wonderful energy around me, start a healing process for the many. That was what I saw my first book would be, to empower my clients to spread their wings. Little did I know, the first step I had to take was a journey into my childhood, peeling the layered onion of my life, and reaching deep into a place I had left behind fifty years ago. Yet for a long time, I wasn't moving that far forward from it. Writing this book has truly been therapeutic for me. Revisiting the past, and making peace with it, was needed. It was time. I can only explore, embrace, and enjoy the rest of my journey forward, to the fullest, once I come to terms with painful parts of my past. I now have the power to do so because I've made peace with it. I embraced that little me, she's no longer in pain. This journey within has been the most humbling gift of life. I embrace it with gratitude. I've become wiser, and I'm emotionally mature because of it.

In the spring of 2011, I listened to Kevin Hall speak at a business conference I attended. He's an inspiring speaker whose book *Aspire* has touched so many hearts and minds, including mine. He dug deeper and discovered the power of words. He suggested that when we embrace and use these words correctly, each can propel us on the paths to lifelong success we deserve. In his book, Hall mentioned an experience he encountered when he was nineteen years old. A friend of his gave him a copy of a classic book entitled *I Dare You!* by William Danforth. The book was originally published during the Great Depression in 1931. The one he held in his hand was the twenty-sixth edition. The middle chapter of the book was about "I Dare You to Build Character" which relates to a story Hall never forgot, about a Hindu legend. Here's how the legend went, as quoted by Hall in his book[17]:

"that at one time all men on earth were gods, but that men so sinned and abused the Divine that Brahma, the god of all gods, decided that the godhead should be taken away from man and hid some place where he would never again find it to abuse it. "We will bury it deep in the earth," said the other gods. "No," said Brahma, "because man will dig down in the earth and find it." "Then we will sink in the deepest ocean," they said. "No," said Brahma, "because man will learn to dive and will find it there, too." "We will hide on the highest mountain," they said. "No," said Brahma, "because man will some day climb every mountain on the earth and again capture the godhead." "Then we do not know where to hide where he cannot find it," said the lesser gods. "I will tell you," said Brahma. "Hide it down in man himself. He will never think to look there." And that is what they did. Hidden down in every man is some of the Divine. Ever since then he has gone the earth digging, diving and climbing, looking for that godlike quality which all the time is hidden down within himself."

I was intrigued by what Hall shared in his book. The calling to take a journey within was getting louder. People say 'there's a time and a place for everything'. When the mind, body and spirit are in harmony with each other, and time, place, and the frame of mind are in perfect alignment, an explosion of possibilities will show up -- can't miss it, and shouldn't. The energy force will be so huge that the only motion to take is onward and upward. That was the force that pushed me forward as I experienced each magical key showing up to open the lock, one by one, and finally a floodgate of opportunity to explore life was present. A new world was in front for me. I have arrived. Now, each day is the first day of the rest of my life.

Lately, I have been wondering, if I could replay the movie of my life – especially the part when I was building my advertising career in Indonesia – and let the *new me* relive it, how would it turn out? This can be another journey worth writing, and sharing.

ℰᏜ

*"Hope is like the sun, which,
as we journey toward it,
casts the shadow of our
burden behind us."*

Samuel Smiles

ℰᏜ

COMING HOME

Life *is* a destination.

When I just started driving, many decades ago, my dad once asked me while I was behind the wheel and about to turn the key. "Do you know where we're going?" he looked at me, a soft smile on his lips. I stared at him in disbelief, not knowing whether he was testing me, or joking with me. But he was calmly serious. I reacted to the question and said, "Of course I do." Just imagine the tone of voice that came with such an answer. He smiled and looked away toward the road and said, "Well then, I can rest assured we'll get there." Silly, I thought. What in the world was that question for? I was puzzled, but never dwelt on it until he was gone. Through my journey of transformation, those words of wisdom had reappeared as if he was giving me his approval that I finally got it. It took me awhile, but I've got it now.

It was a destination my dad was asking me whether I knew where we were going. It is now. That was another moment of clarity for me. I was going in circles for a very long time because

I didn't have a destination. I didn't have a purpose in life, not even a worthwhile intention. I was never at home, never here present in the now. I plugged away accomplishing tasks and before long it became a dull process. I wasn't content regardless of how many tasks I completed and how successful each was. And then one day I stopped, looked back, and wondered how I got where I was. I am now a participant of life. I am on the train of life by choice. I make it my choice to make from life. This train will make some stops. I can get off and explore each stop, and get back on until it reaches its destination. I will celebrate that destination, and then start another journey as opportunity opens up.

The trip to Pittsburg, finding Josephine, was a divine validation of the journey I had been taking that finally brought me here. I was given a chance to experience a new me. I am here now. I am no longer too busy to notice life. When we were back from that two-week vacation exploring Kansas, Georgia and South Carolina, we came home with a new me. Happiness is here. I can now look back with gratitude for the person I have become. I have learned much about me and my life. I can't describe the feeling I have now, in words, but I can feel it -- the excitement of life, the energy that purposefully pulls me forward. I feel the calmness and peace with every breath. It's amazingly delightful. This is how contentment feels. You, too, will know when it comes to you. You can't force it to come. You can't fake it as if it's already here. You will feel it when it arrives. Flow with life. Continue to renew your relationship with life; be curious about it, get to know it, and understand it. It doesn't bite. And your partnership with it will flourish.

Halfway into my course with IIN®, Joshua Rosenthal, our inspiring teacher, asked this one question that has since been a beam of light in my mind, "Where do you see yourself *beyond* this course?" I have been playing with this signature question a lot, listening to it in my head. As I'm doing so, I can see myself expanding into the future. Where do I see myself beyond this book? Where do I see myself beyond this interview, beyond today, this weekend, this trip, this event, beyond meeting this client? And suddenly, I can see my clients' journeys expanding beyond the day they came to me. There must be something that brought them to me, something that made our paths cross. They were searching, for a life's change, for expansion. I encourage you to continue asking valuable questions to expand, to be curious about you, about life. Deepak Chopra said it beautifully, "live in the questions, and life will move you into the answers." I continue living life with an inquisitive mind, I ask questions, I explore, I search. And I continue to enjoy, and embrace what comes. Most importantly, I embrace me. I'm home.

You will be too.

ဨၚ

*"If you get the inside right,
the outside will fall into place.
Primary reality is within;
secondary reality without."*

Eckhart Tolle
The Power of Now:
A Guide to
Spiritual Enlightenment

ဨ ၚ

THOUGHTS TO PONDER

One of the precious exercises I learned during the course at the Institute for Integrative Nutrition® was *Morning Pages,* introduced by Julia Cameron. In that spirit, I'd like to offer these next questions to help you start finding your life's voice. Go to a place of quiet and peace, and let the pen roll.

1. Take a journey back to your childhood, what memory do you remember? What was painful? What was happy?

_____

_____

_____

_____

_____

_____

_____

_____

_____

_____

_____

_____

_____

2. What are you thankful for, for the person you have now become?

_____

_____

_____

_____

_____

_____

_____

_____

_____

_____

_____

_____

_____

_____

_____

_____

_____

_____

_____

3. *Disregard all the obstacles and excuses, how do you see yourself beyond this point? What is possible?*

_____

_____

_____

_____

_____

_____

_____

_____

_____

_____

_____

_____

_____

_____

_____

_____

_____

_____

_____

_____

_____

Inge Maskun

෯෮

*"Our stories hold unique
inspiration for one another."*

Lailah Gifty Akita
Beautiful Quotes

෮෯

INSPIRED TO SHARE?

If you hear the calling to express your thoughts, stories, or share your journey of self-discovery, please visit:

www.embraceableme.com

I appreciate your courage to inspire and strengthen others.

I appreciate you!

To learn more about my Health Coaching services -- how I can guide, support, and empower you to reach your *destination*, and how you can take advantage of a *free* Wellness Discovery session with me -- please contact me through: www.ingemaskun.com

Inge Maskun

ENDNOTES

[1] Gregoire, Carolyn. "16 Signs You're A Little (Or A Lot) Type A." *The Huffington Post*. TheHuffingtonPost.com, Inc. 13 Jan. 2014. Web. 16 Mar 2015.

[2] Servando, Kristine. "Advertising writer dies after '30-hour shift' at global agency in Indonesia." *South China Morning Post*. South China Morning Post Publishers Ltd. 19 Dec. 2013. Web. 16 Mar 2015.

[3] http://www.asiaworkstraining.com

[4] Morton, Julia F. "Mangosteen". *Fruits of Warm Climates*. Miami: Julia F. Morton, 1987. p. 301–304. (Purdue University, Center for New Crops & Plant Products.) Web. 19 Mar 2015.

[5] http://www.exploremymangosteen.com

[6] Johnsen, Kurt. Yoga For Life. http://www.zliving.com/tv/yoga-life-14766/ *ZLiving*. Web. 19 Mar 2015.

[7] Hill, Napoleon. *Think and Grow Rich*. New York: Barnes & Noble, Inc., 2008. p. 169. Print.

[8] http://www.tm.org

[9] A *kebaya* is a traditional blouse-dress combination that originates from Indonesia and is worn by women in Indonesia, Malaysia, Brunei, Burma, Singapore, southern Thailand, Cambodia and the southern part of the Philippines. Wikipedia: en.wikipedia.org/wiki/Kebaya. Web. 30 Mar 2015.

[10] A length of *batik* measuring 2.5m x 1m (98" x 39.5") is known as a *kain panjang* and is primarily (and traditionally) used as a garment to cover the lower body (of women). Djumena, Nian S. *Batik and Its Kind*. Jakarta: Djambatan, 1990. p. 51. Print.

[11] Grout, Pam. *E-Squared: Nine Do-It-Yourself Energy Experiments that Prove your Thoughts Create your Reality.* p. 27. United States of America: Hay House, Inc., 2013. Print.

[12] For more info regarding Institute for Integrative Nutrition®, visit http://geti.in/1ATQoHO

[13] Felitti, Vicent J. *Forward.* The Impact of Early Life Trauma on Health and Disease: The Hidden Epidemic. The United Kingdom: Cambridge University Press, 2010. eBook. Web. 31 Mar. 2015.

[14] Godin, Seth. "Tenacity is not the same as persistence." *Seth's Blog.* TypePad. 2 Nov. 2013. Web. 31 Mar.2015.

[15] Morning Pages was first introduced in *The Artist's Way* by Julia Cameron, author of books, plays and film. This exercise helped me recover and discover my inner voice, creativity, and purpose through a 3-page daily free writing exercise, which brought me to writing the book you now have in hands.

[16] Sambal is chili based sauce made of ground chilies. Other ingredients added to it are shallot, salt, sugar, shrimp paste, and lime. There are various sambal recipes based on individual preference and creativity.

[17] Hall, Kevin. *Aspire.* New York City: Harper Collins, 2010. p. 44. Print.

Inge Maskun

&CR

*"If search is on
for finding the real friend,
then make sure
one's journey on this path
is never ending."*

Anuj Somany

&CB

GRATITUDE

Four months ago, when I started typing a few sentences that marked the beginning of this book, I got butterflies in my stomach. As I'm now wrapping up this first writing journey, my mind and soul continue to explore possibilities, and my heart dances in solemn gratitude for the magnitude of support and encouragement I've received, and continues pouring in. You all are my true and dear friends. I'm forever grateful!

~IIN® Teachers and Staff for nurturing my mind, body and spirit with the wisdom of health, and empowering me to guide and support my family, friends and clients to claim their health and own their future. Joshua Rosenthal, bless your heart!!

~The fearless and committed Joshua Rosenthal, Lindsey Smith, Launch Your Dream Book Ambassadors, fellow authors, and peer coaches for your encouraging support, notes and comments, which pop up on the wall 24/7. You're immensely appreciated.

~Toastmasters International for your valuable programs that continue training me to organize my thoughts, and helping me build my competence. To fellow Toastmasters for your weekly support, feedback and friendship that strengthen my confidence.

~My two Believing Mirrors, Jude Ling and Donna Sletten; the words 'Thank You' aren't big enough to hold the amount of gratitude I have for the unlimited time, focus, guidance, and friendship you have made available to me (even when you were on your vacation, Donna!). You both walked my journey with me! (P.S. Mrs. Ling, "I *know* I will do it all over again, with you!" P.P.S. Tom and Casey Ling, thank you for gracefully giving me the space in your home for hours of editing).

~My H.B. for calming me down when I'm nervous or worried, for saying *yes* to growing and expanding our minds, for going through each line of the stories I write, and for your continued love and trust in me and my dreams.

~Last but not least – LIFE -- for continuing to challenge me, teach me, honor me, embrace me, pull me forward, and open my mind to abundant possibilities. Most importantly, for leading me with your music. I love you!

Charlie and Inge. Atlanta, Nov. 2014.

Inge Maskun

Onward and Upward!

35258650R00099

Made in the USA
Middletown, DE
25 September 2016